Can I Keep It?
Small Pets Guide

Can I Keep It? Small Pets Guide

CompanionHouse Books™ is an imprint of Fox Chapel Publishing.

Project Team
Editor: Amy Deputato
Copy Editor: Colleen Dorsey
Design: Mary Ann Kahn
Translator: Donna Vekteris
Technical Reviewer: Thomas Mazorlig

Project Team (French edition)
Editorial Directors: Isabelle Jeuge-Maynart and Ghislaine Stora
Editor: Aurélie Starckmann
Graphic Design: Aurore Élie
Layout and Cover: Anna Bardon
Production: Donia Faiz

ISBN 978-1-62008-391-8

Library of Congress Cataloging-in-Publication Data
Title: Can I keep it? : small pets guide / editor, Amy Deputato.
Description: Mount Joy, PA : Fox Chapel Publishers International Ltd.,
    [2020] | Audience: Ages 8 to 13 | Audience: Grades 4-6 | Summary: "The
    author presents 39 pets, many of them considered "exotic," and discusses
    what makes these pets unique, where they come from, and how to care for
    them, including proper habitat and feeding"-- Provided by publisher.
Identifiers: LCCN 2019050702 (print) | LCCN 2019050703 (ebook) | ISBN
    9781620083918 (paperback) | ISBN 9781620083925 (ebook)
Subjects: LCSH: Pets--Juvenile literature. | Pets--Miscellanea--Juvenile
    literature. | Pets--Size--Juvenile literature. | Deputato, Amy, editor.
Classification: LCC SF416.2 .C347 2020 (print) | LCC SF416.2 (ebook) |
    DDC 636.088/7--dc23
LC record available at https://lccn.loc.gov/2019050702
LC ebook record available at https://lccn.loc.gov/2019050703

Fox Chapel Publishing
903 Square Street
Mount Joy, PA 17552

www.facebook.com/companionhousebooks

We are always looking for talented authors. To submit an idea, please send a brief inquiry to acquisitions@foxchapelpublishing.com.

Printed and bound in Singapore
23 22 21 20   2 4 6 8 10 9 7 5 3 1

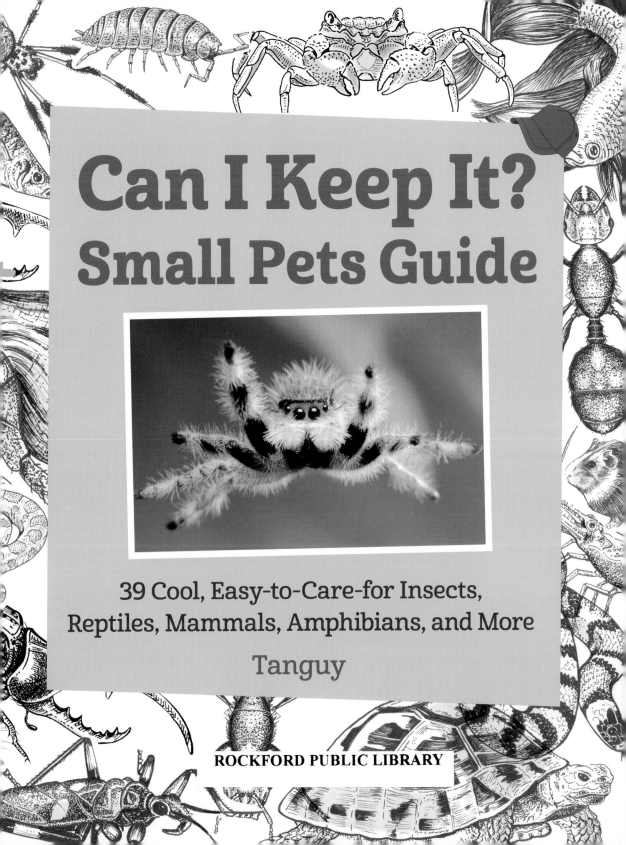

Can I Keep It?
Small Pets Guide

39 Cool, Easy-to-Care-for Insects,
Reptiles, Mammals, Amphibians, and More

Tanguy

PREFACE

Adopting an animal is a big responsibility. Whether you have a family of woodlice or a single rodent, you need to be able to care for them every day and have a budget for their care. Your pet may live a long time, depending on the species, and when you adopt an animal, you have to be ready to take care of that animal for its entire life.

Never buy an animal without first making a careful decision. You need to really think about it and have a plan for different situations: Will everyone who lives with you welcome the pet? Who will take care of the pet when you go on vacation? Can you afford veterinarian fees if your pet is sick or injured? These are just a few examples, and you must have answers to these questions—before your pet comes home!

The animals in this book are easy to raise, on two conditions: that you learn as much as possible about them before deciding to keep them, and that you take time to make a plan for how you will raise them.

So, if you love animals, are naturally curious, and enjoy a little DIY, you'll discover that raising these unusual creatures in your home is a real adventure!

TANGUY

CAUTION!

The skin of most amphibians secretes some type of chemical as a defense mechanism; some are more potent than others. These secretions could cause inflammation of the eyes, mouth, or other mucous membranes. Thus, it's best to handle amphibians only when necessary and always wash your hands after handling your pet. Alternatively, you can wear moistened unpowdered latex gloves to handle your amphibian pet.

Reptiles and amphibians can also carry *Salmonella*, so, again, hand-washing is important after handling your pet or any of its equipment.

CONTENTS

VAMPIRE CRAB
Geosesarma sp.

INDONESIA

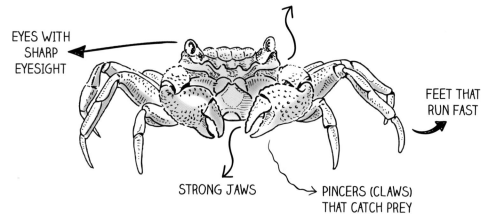

CEPHALOTHORAX (FUSED HEAD AND CHEST AREA)

EYES WITH SHARP EYESIGHT

FEET THAT RUN FAST

STRONG JAWS

PINCERS (CLAWS) THAT CATCH PREY

ORIGIN

Vampire crabs, *Geosesarma* sp., come from Indonesia. These charming little crustaceans are found on Java, Sulawesi, and many other small islands. They live near sources of fresh water in the hot, humid, tropical jungle. These crabs come in as many different colors as there are valleys on some of these islands, and many species have not even been discovered or officially named yet!

Vampire crabs are gaining popularity as pets with beginners because more and more people are becoming fascinated by the interesting looks and behavior of these unusual creatures. *Geosesarma aedituens, G. albomita, G. amphinome, G. angustifrons, G. araneum,* and *G. aurantium* are just a few examples of the fifty species that we already know about.

LOOK AT THESE COOL COLORS!

BEHAVIOR

We don't know a lot about how vampire crabs live in the wild, but we have figured out a few things:

- They live and reproduce near fresh water, unlike many other crabs, who need brackish (partially salty) water.

- They don't live in the water. They do go into the water sometimes, but they spend most of their time on the riverbanks, where they dig tunnels.

- They climb branches and tree trunks really well, most often at night, when they are hunting.

- They are very good hunters and can easily catch small crickets.

- They give birth to live young, meaning that their babies do not hatch from eggs and don't have a larval stage—they are simply born as tiny versions of their parents. But it takes a few months for their beautiful colors to appear.

MY OBSERVATIONS
At first, your crabs will be shy and only come out of their hiding places at night. Be patient. With time, they will get used to their new home, and you'll be able to watch them exploring their tank during the daytime.

HOUSING

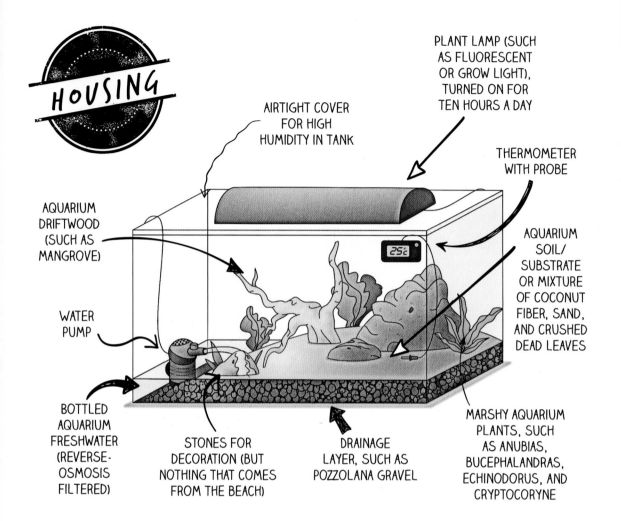

PLANT LAMP (SUCH AS FLUORESCENT OR GROW LIGHT), TURNED ON FOR TEN HOURS A DAY

AIRTIGHT COVER FOR HIGH HUMIDITY IN TANK

THERMOMETER WITH PROBE

AQUARIUM DRIFTWOOD (SUCH AS MANGROVE)

AQUARIUM SOIL/ SUBSTRATE OR MIXTURE OF COCONUT FIBER, SAND, AND CRUSHED DEAD LEAVES

WATER PUMP

25°C

BOTTLED AQUARIUM FRESHWATER (REVERSE-OSMOSIS FILTERED)

STONES FOR DECORATION (BUT NOTHING THAT COMES FROM THE BEACH)

DRAINAGE LAYER, SUCH AS POZZOLANA GRAVEL

MARSHY AQUARIUM PLANTS, SUCH AS ANUBIAS, BUCEPHALANDRAS, ECHINODORUS, AND CRYPTOCORYNE

◆ Vampire crabs adapt easily to life in captivity, just like all of the other species in this book. They will live happily in a properly set-up paludarium (a tank with both land and water elements) where they can thrive as a family. They live in groups, so start off with at least a couple—a group of four or six crabs is even better! It's easy to tell whether they are male or female by the size of their abdomens, so ask the store where you purchase yours to give you an even mix.

◆ They live at 77° Fahrenheit (25° Celsius), so if your lighting doesn't heat up the tank enough, buy a small heater to place next to or underneath the paludarium.

You must always monitor the temperature, so you'll need a small probe thermometer, which is a very useful and inexpensive tool.

◆ Your crabs need a very humid atmosphere in their tank. A glass or plexiglass lid on top of the tank will keep the humidity high, ensuring that the crabs and the plants in the tank will thrive. Every time you open the tank to feed your crabs, you will refresh the air inside the tank.

◆ Adding a small pump for the water in the tank will keep the water clean and balanced.

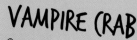

THIS CRAB IS
REALLY SHY!

CARE TIPS

Taking care of vampire crabs is very simple: just feed them regularly, add water to the tank when the water level is low, and clean the glass from time to time with a paper towel and a few drops of white vinegar. (I advise using reverse-osmosis filtered water in the tank.)

FEEDING

• Crabs are opportunistic feeders, meaning that they eat whenever they can. A basic diet of specially formulated crab food (such as Hikari "Crab Cuisine") will be perfect. Put some of the pellets in a small dish or bottle cap in the tank, and they won't hesitate to come and eat! Put a little bit of water in the dish when you serve the food, because the pellets are easier for the crabs to eat when they are slightly damp.

• You can also feed your crabs small live crickets from time to time. The crabs will quickly go off to hunt for their meal!

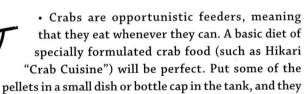

• Put a small cuttlefish bone in one corner of the tank to allow them to come nibble and get some calcium. The crabs need the calcium to be able to molt (shed their skin)—yes, crabs molt!

• If all goes well, a bunch of baby crabs will appear in your tank a few weeks after you bring your adult couple home. Leave all of them in the tank together. If the parents are properly fed, they won't be tempted to eat their offspring!

COCKROACH

Family Blaberidae and Corydiidae

NOTE: EXOTIC TROPICAL COCKROACHES ARE ILLEGAL TO KEEP IN FLORIDA; REGULATIONS IN OTHER STATES VARY BY SPECIES, BUT SOME SPECIES, INCLUDING THE DOMINO COCKROACH, ARE LEGAL TO KEEP WITHOUT A PERMIT

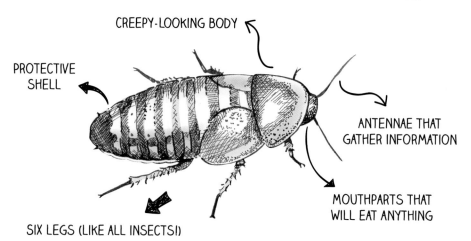

EVERYWHERE ON THE PLANET EXCEPT THE NORTH AND SOUTH POLES

CREEPY-LOOKING BODY

PROTECTIVE SHELL

ANTENNAE THAT GATHER INFORMATION

MOUTHPARTS THAT WILL EAT ANYTHING

SIX LEGS (LIKE ALL INSECTS!)

ORIGIN

Disgusting! That's often the first word that comes to mind when people see a cockroach. But I disagree! Cockroaches are not disgusting at all. These charming insects are woodland animals that live in the humus (decaying plant and animal matter) layer of the forest floor. Once people get over their initial reaction, they realize that these are amazing creatures that also look like they're from outer space!

There are hundreds of species of cockroaches on the planet. Some measure just a few millimeters (less than a quarter-inch) in length. Others, such as the rhinoceros cockroach (which lives in Australia), is a real giant and can grow to more than 3 inches (8 cm) long and weigh 1¼ ounces (35 grams). A real beast!

Some species come in very pretty colors, such as *Therea petiveriana*, commonly known as the domino cockroach.

- Roaches are basically nocturnal, meaning that they sleep during the day and are awake at night.

- They live in groups and multiply easily in the right conditions. A female will lay oothecas, which are sort of "egg cases." Mrs. Roach then buries them in the substrate of the tank. If you allow the eggs to "cook" at the right temperature and humidity level, in a few weeks you may find a batch of mini-cockroaches, just a few millimeters long, that look just like their parents.

- Cockroaches molt (shed their skin) regularly from birth into adulthood. They do not have wings.

- Madagascar hissing cockroaches, *Gromphadorhina portentosa*, are the perfect choice for your first cockroach pets. They're big and beautiful and they have the fascinating habit of hissing when you touch them, which can take you by surprise at first.

MY OBSERVATIONS
Cardboard egg trays are the perfect places for raising cockroaches. Stack them with some space between each tray so your roaches can hide between the layers.

HOUSING

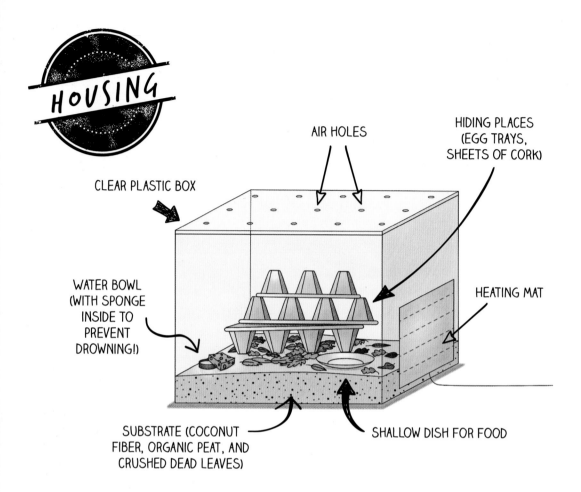

AIR HOLES

HIDING PLACES (EGG TRAYS, SHEETS OF CORK)

CLEAR PLASTIC BOX

WATER BOWL (WITH SPONGE INSIDE TO PREVENT DROWNING!)

HEATING MAT

SUBSTRATE (COCONUT FIBER, ORGANIC PEAT, AND CRUSHED DEAD LEAVES)

SHALLOW DISH FOR FOOD

◆ Cockroaches are easy to raise and keep in captivity, and the common species are affordable to buy. Thanks to people who love to breed and raise roaches, you can now find dozens of species available.

◆ You can start off with a small group of adults that will quickly start a family if you take good care of them.

◆ Most cockroach species like warmth (about 79 to 81° Fahrenheit [26 to 27° Celsius]), so keep them near a radiator, place a lamp with a heating bulb near their home, or place a small heating mat on one side of their home. Whatever you use, be sure to monitor the temperature with a small, inexpensive digital thermometer. This is important!

◆ Remember to pierce tiny air holes in the enclosure. Make a lot of holes but be sure they're very small so that the baby cockroaches can't get out (although there's not much risk that they will start living in your bedroom, because the temperature will not be warm enough for them).

◆ Pile up the egg trays to make hiding places. You can add one or two trays without any space between them for the baby roaches to hide in. They will appreciate this type of confinement, which will make them feel safe.

CARE TIPS

Depending on the species, roaches like a little humidity. Be sure to get the right information for the species you choose to keep. To add humidity to their environment, spray a little water on one side of the enclosure only, so that they still have a dry corner to go to if they wish.

FEEDING

- When it comes to eating, cockroaches will try pretty much anything you offer them. From your leftover pizza to organic vegetables, they will eat it all! But I suggest that you feed more fruits and vegetables (carrots, oranges, apples) than chicken nuggets and burgers.

- Toss a little dry dog or cat food into their enclosure; the extra protein is good for them.

- Cockroaches like a clean environment. Place their food in a small, shallow dish so that fruits and vegetables don't rot in the substrate.

MILLIPEDE

Family Julidae

NOTE: THE GIANT AFRICAN MILLIPEDE IS ILLEGAL IN FLORIDA; CERTAIN SPECIES REQUIRE USDA PERMIT; ILLEGAL IN CANADA

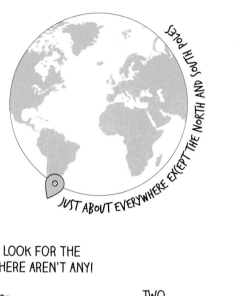

JUST ABOUT EVERYWHERE EXCEPT THE NORTH AND SOUTH POLES

BODY THAT LOOKS LIKE A LITTLE SAUSAGE ON LEGS

DON'T LOOK FOR THE EYES – THERE AREN'T ANY!

TWO ANTENNAE THAT GATHER INFORMATION

TOO MANY LEGS TO COUNT

MOUTHPARTS THAT CRUNCH ON PLANTS AND DEAD WOOD

ORIGIN

Millipedes belong to the the class of diplopods. *Millipede* means "a thousand feet," but that description isn't really accurate. They have a lot of feet, but definitely fewer than a thousand—although I've never counted them!

There are many different species of millipede. Some are just around an inch (2 to 3 centimeters) long, while others are giants, measuring almost 8 inches (20 cm) in length. Here are two popular species being raised in captivity:

• *Tonkinbolus dollfusi:* This is a small, very colorful millipede that comes from southeast Asia. I see them often in Thailand, and they're really cute.

• *Mardonius parilis parilis:* This one's a lot bigger but not huge. It lives in a slightly drier environment than other species and is native to Africa.

- Millipedes like humidity. They live in the layer of humus (decaying matter) on the forest floor and may only come out from under their layer of dead leaves after it rains or on very humid days.

- Millipedes have an important role in nature. They are detrivores; this means, depending on the species, that they eat dead leaves, rotting plants, and even wood, which they transform into humus that helps trees grow.

- Millipedes grow as they molt (shed their skin). Each time a millipede molts, a new ring appears on its body.

- The millipede is a harmless creature, and it has two ways to protect itself:
  1. Plan A: It curls up in a tight spiral, like a roll of licorice.

  2. Plan B: If the predator is too persistent, the millipede releases an orange-colored, bad-smelling secretion. You'd better wash your hands well if you're the victim! You'll have the odor on you for a few days. (Some people are allergic to this substance and can have an itchy skin reaction.)

MY OBSERVATIONS

Even though the orange substance that millipedes release when they are stressed is far from dangerous, avoid getting it near your mouth, just to be safe. After handling your millipede, wash your hands thoroughly with soap.

HOUSING

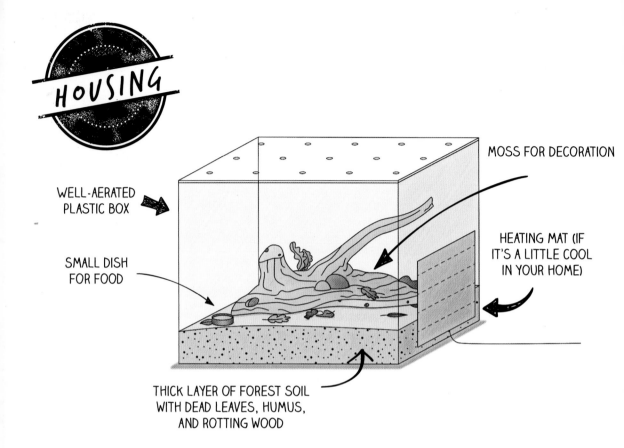

WELL-AERATED PLASTIC BOX

MOSS FOR DECORATION

SMALL DISH FOR FOOD

HEATING MAT (IF IT'S A LITTLE COOL IN YOUR HOME)

THICK LAYER OF FOREST SOIL WITH DEAD LEAVES, HUMUS, AND ROTTING WOOD

◆ I think that millipedes are some of the easiest animals to raise. They don't need fancy housing: a clear plastic storage box, like one you'd use for clothes, will do nicely. Pierce holes in the lid to give them enough air. They like humidity but not stale air.

◆ Next, collect some earth from the forest floor. This is important. I do not recommend peat, garden soil, or coconut fiber. Lay a thick layer of forest soil on the bottom of the box, at least 2 to 2½ inches (5 to 6 cm) deep. Spray water over only half of the area in the box so that the millipedes have a choice of moist or fairly dry substrate.

◆ Most millipedes you'll find are tropical species, often African or Asian, so you'll need to maintain their environment at a temperature of at least 77° Fahrenheit (25° Celsius). To do this, you can place their home near a radiator (**near, but not against,** the radiator, which will kill them in no time!).

◆ If you can't achieve the right temperature, another option for heating is a small, low-wattage heating mat made for reptiles. Place it on one side of your box and monitor the temperature (a small digital thermometer is your friend!). Do not place the heating mat under the box. This will heat the substrate too much, causing too much condensation (moisture) on the lid, which is not good.

MILLIPEDE

CARE TIPS

Remember to spray half of the substrate often to maintain an adequate level of humidity.

FEEDING

- When you purchase your millipede, be sure to ask about proper feeding for your particular species. This is important.

- Depending on the species, millipedes will eat either vegetables (e.g., salad greens, carrot peels) or rotting wood that you collect from the forest floor. You will need to replace vegetables regularly, before they start to rot.

EGYPTIAN PREDATOR BEETLE

Anthia sexmaculata

EGYPT

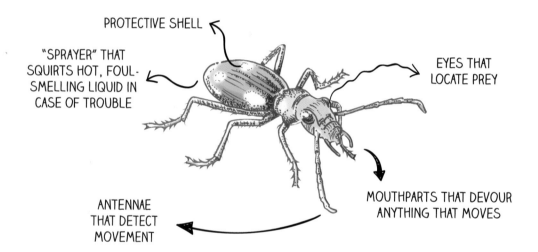

PROTECTIVE SHELL

"SPRAYER" THAT SQUIRTS HOT, FOUL-SMELLING LIQUID IN CASE OF TROUBLE

EYES THAT LOCATE PREY

ANTENNAE THAT DETECT MOVEMENT

MOUTHPARTS THAT DEVOUR ANYTHING THAT MOVES

ORIGIN

This is one impressive creature. It may be small, but it is a powerful predator. Believe me, if you were a little insect, you would not want to cross paths with one of these!

This insect, whose scientific name is *Anthia sexmaculata*, is a ground beetle in the family *Carabidae*. This family includes more than 500 species! We will focus on this particular beetle, because it is one of the easiest to find from specialty sellers.

20

BEHAVIOR

This beetle is amazing in many ways.

- First, it is an outstanding hunter that is quick to go after its prey by chasing it, which makes it very interesting to watch.

- Next, it is very pretty, with its black-and-white body on long legs.

- Finally—and I have saved the best for last—this animal has astonished researchers for a long time because of its unique defense mechanism. Its body has two storage chambers at the back that contain different chemicals. When these chemicals combine, they set off an explosion! The beetle squirts a hot, irritating liquid that is guaranteed to stop a predator in its tracks.

I don't recommend this pet for a child younger than ten, but it should be fine for a responsible older child.

MY OBSERVATIONS
This beetle is fairly easy to raise, but beware: it's best observed with the eyes, not with the hands.

HOUSING

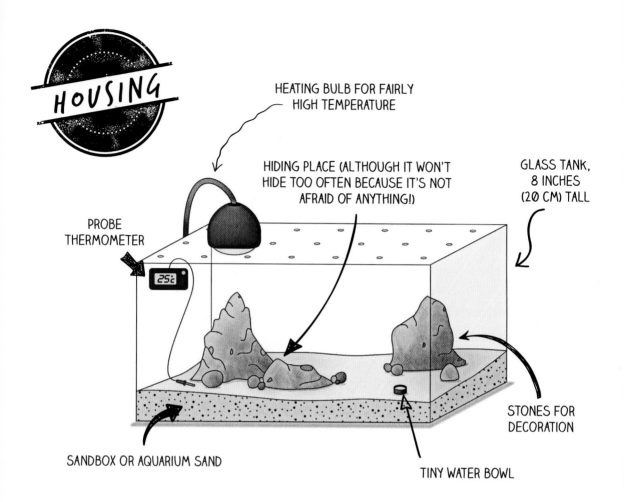

HEATING BULB FOR FAIRLY HIGH TEMPERATURE

HIDING PLACE (ALTHOUGH IT WON'T HIDE TOO OFTEN BECAUSE IT'S NOT AFRAID OF ANYTHING!)

GLASS TANK, 8 INCHES (20 CM) TALL

PROBE THERMOMETER

25℃

STONES FOR DECORATION

SANDBOX OR AQUARIUM SAND

TINY WATER BOWL

◆ This insect is native to the very dry regions of Egypt. It's easy to create this hot and dry environment in its tank.

◆ The predator beetle cannot climb glass walls, so a small aquarium that is 8 inches (20 cm) high will do the job.

◆ Add a layer of sand about an inch (2 to 3 cm) deep as well as some stones for decoration. Be sure to sit the stones firmly in the bottom of the aquarium to prevent your beetle from digging underneath the stones and accidentally being crushed.

◆ Place a lamp over the tank on one side so that the tank has a hot side and a cooler side. This way, if it is too hot in the area under the lamp (about 77° Fahrenheit [25° Celsius]), your beetle can seek refuge at the other end of the tank.

◆ Add a mini water dish: a plastic bottle cap set into the sand works well.

CARE TIPS

As I've explained, this beetle can squirt a corrosive substance, so be careful not to get any on your hands or, worse, in your eyes. I strongly recommend that you don't touch the beetle, also because it might bite or pinch you. To move your beetle, use a small plastic container or glass. Hold the container sideways and give your beetle a gentle little push with a ballpoint pen to get it inside.

FEEDING

- This small but tough little predator will attack and eat pretty much anything that moves.

- Grasshoppers, caterpillars, worms, crickets, and other insects are ideal meals.

- You can usually buy mealworms or small crickets at a pet-supply store. Your beetle will truly enjoy them.

- Feed your beetle three or four times a week. If it ever doesn't go after its prey because it isn't hungry, which might be the case, remove the food and try again a few days later.

SUN BEETLE

Pachnoda marginata

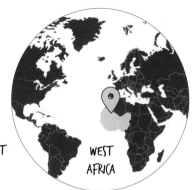

WEST AFRICA

NOTE: REQUIRES USDA PERMIT AND APPROVED CONTAINMENT

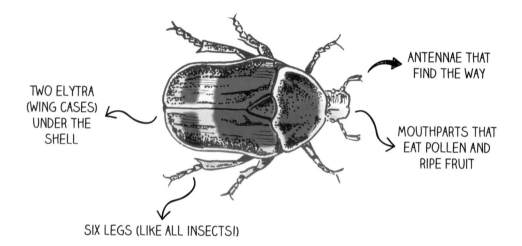

ANTENNAE THAT FIND THE WAY

TWO ELYTRA (WING CASES) UNDER THE SHELL

MOUTHPARTS THAT EAT POLLEN AND RIPE FRUIT

SIX LEGS (LIKE ALL INSECTS!)

ORIGIN

This beetle is found in many countries in Africa, including Mali, Senegal, Chad, and Sudan. The adult beetle colonizes, or takes over, "host" plants, such as the mango tree and the cotton plant. It lives on pollen and fruit.

THE YELLOW-AND-BLACK SHELL AND ELYTRA (WING CASES) HIDE TWO WINGS!

BEHAVIOR

- The sun beetle's life span is about seven months. This species is really interesting to observe because its appearance changes completely over its life cycle.

- It starts as an egg, from which a larva will hatch. The larva will spend the first few months of its life helping dead wood decompose underground, using its powerful mouthparts, or mandibles (don't panic—your fingers are safe!). This kind of animal is called a *decomposer*. The larva will grow to about 1¼ to 1½ inches (3 to 4 cm) in length. It will then enclose itself in a type of hard cocoon and transform into the next stage, called a *pupa*, that looks like a creature from outer space!

- The pupal stage takes a few weeks, and there is really nothing to see because everything takes place inside the cocoon. One day, the pupa will transform into a beetle, and out of the cocoon will come this colorful little flying insect that will live about two months before it dies. Before this happens, it will lay eggs in the ground, which will become the next generation.

- It's amazing when you think about it! It's born underground, eating wood, and it ends up flying to eat the pollen on flowers!

MY OBSERVATIONS

Buy your first larvae in a reptile store. These larvae are used to feed reptiles, which adore them, and they are not expensive.

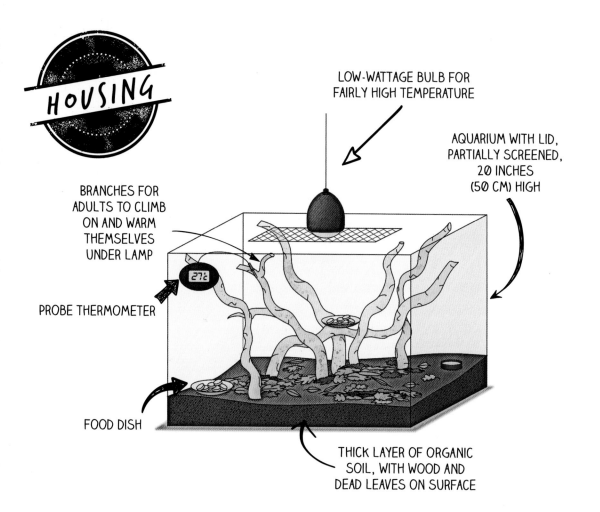

HOUSING

LOW-WATTAGE BULB FOR
FAIRLY HIGH TEMPERATURE

AQUARIUM WITH LID,
PARTIALLY SCREENED,
20 INCHES
(50 CM) HIGH

BRANCHES FOR
ADULTS TO CLIMB
ON AND WARM
THEMSELVES
UNDER LAMP

27℃

PROBE THERMOMETER

FOOD DISH

THICK LAYER OF ORGANIC
SOIL, WITH WOOD AND
DEAD LEAVES ON SURFACE

◆ There's nothing too hard about raising this insect, which is easy to keep in an aquarium. All you need is a thick layer of organic soil (always damp but never wet), at least 4 inches (10 cm) deep, and some crushed dead leaves and dead wood you've collected from the woods.

◆ A low-wattage bulb to reach a temperature of 79 to 81° Fahrenheit (26 to 27° Celsius) in the aquarium, a lid with either holes in it or a screen for air, and a few branches for the adults to perch on help complete a simple but very comfortable home.

CARE TIPS
Change your mixture of soil, wood, and leaves every three to four months to help new generations of larvae grow properly. At the end of a few months, after raising some larvae, you will find beetles in all stages: adults, growing larvae, pupae—a beetle factory in your bedroom!

FEEDING

- When it comes to food, these insects love ripe fruit, like bananas, as well as flower pollen, which you will find in health-food stores. Change the fruit regularly to prevent mold from growing in the food dish.

- You can also give your beetles royal jelly (a substance produced by honey bees to feed queen bees) from time to time. They love it.

- There's no need for a water bowl. Your beetles will get enough drinking water when you spray the substrate.

MOUSE

Mus musculus

EVERYWHERE ON THE PLANET EXCEPT THE NORTH AND SOUTH POLES

EARS THAT HEAR VERY WELL

WHISKERS, ACTUALLY CALLED VIBRISSAE

TAIL THAT HELPS IT BALANCE

INCISORS THAT GNAW ON EVERYTHING

FEET THAT RUN, CLIMB, DIG, AND HOLD FOOD

ORIGIN

People have a lot of opinions about this little rodent! Some people are crazy about mice (I personally love them), but other people don't like them at all. Mice are some of the oldest rodents in the world. They love to sneak around our homes, looking for food that they can get into.

There are many species, but the common gray or white "house mouse" is *Mus musculus*. Breeders have created a wide variety of colors and coat types, including the red-eyed albino and the long-haired angora.

BEHAVIOR

Before you think about welcoming a mouse into your home—and this is the truth—you must know that mice can stink! The smell can be really awful and will even sting your eyes if you don't change the litter often enough. Now that I've warned you...

- The mouse is a great little pet that is easy to raise as long as you provide the right living conditions.

- A mouse is a cute animal, it likes to play, it doesn't take up too much space, and it lives for about two years. It can be a great companion.

- Mice are active mostly during the daytime and evening.

- A mouse is not a good pet for young children because its tiny size makes it fragile.

- If you choose a female mouse, make sure that she has not had any contact with male mice—or else you may be surprised with a litter of baby mice after you bring her home!

MY OBSERVATIONS

Mice are social animals. They live in small groups. Because they produce a lot of babies, I suggest you start by adopting two females. That way, you won't suddenly find yourself raising a large family! Plus, females don't smell as bad as males do.

HOUSING

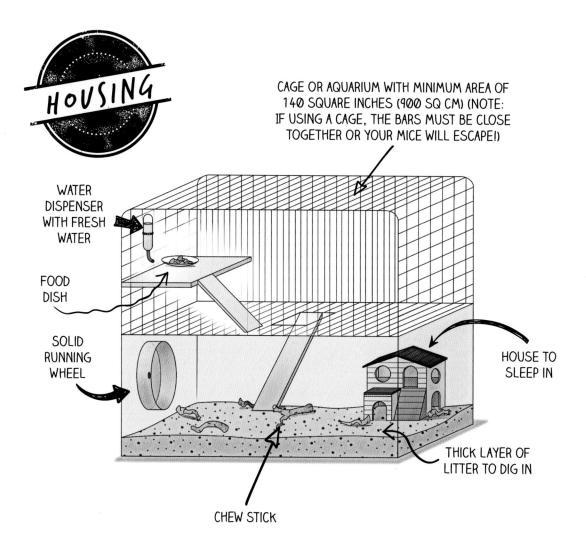

CAGE OR AQUARIUM WITH MINIMUM AREA OF 140 SQUARE INCHES (900 SQ CM) (NOTE: IF USING A CAGE, THE BARS MUST BE CLOSE TOGETHER OR YOUR MICE WILL ESCAPE!)

WATER DISPENSER WITH FRESH WATER

FOOD DISH

SOLID RUNNING WHEEL

HOUSE TO SLEEP IN

THICK LAYER OF LITTER TO DIG IN

CHEW STICK

◆ Keep your mice in a large cage or an aquarium with a screened top so they cannot escape.

◆ Mice don't like drafts. They also have sensitive skin and lungs, so choose high-quality litter. Do not use wood shavings, because once your mice urinate on them, the shavings give off a substance called *phenol*, and that's not good for your pets' small lungs. Hemp, flax, corncob bedding, and coconut fiber are good choices.

◆ Your mice need a wheel because they need to run, but do not get a wheel with bars. Their tails could get trapped in between the bars, so get a solid wheel.

◆ Get a small house—but not one made of wood—to put inside the cage. A wooden house will start to stink very quickly and give off phenol due to the urine. Do not put cotton balls inside the house, because they are very dangerous if the mice eat them. Instead, use an old (but clean!) sock that you can either wash regularly or throw out, or buy a cozy bed made for rodents.

CARE TIPS

Be patient when getting to know your mice. Offer them treats, like dried fruit, from your hand and never catch them by their tails. They will soon learn to trust you.

FEEDING

- Mice are omnivorous, which means that they eat both meat- and plant-based foods.

- Mixed seeds, dried fruit, a little high-quality dry dog or cat food, dried insects, and some rodent pellets make a very good diet.

- Change their food as well as the water in the dispenser every day. Change their litter at least twice a week.

RAT

Genus Rattus

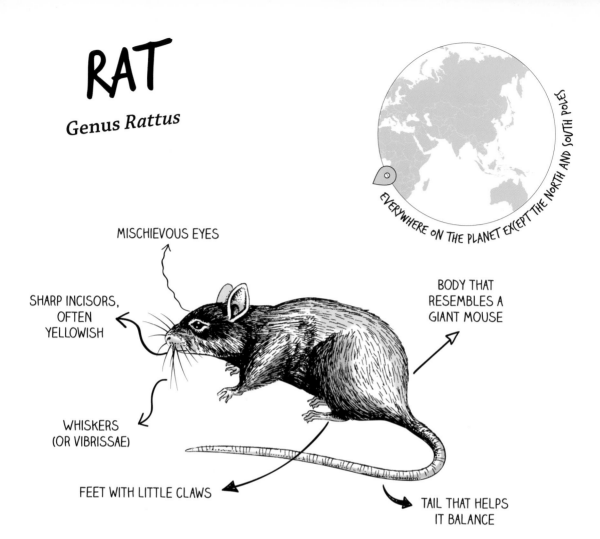

EVERYWHERE ON THE PLANET EXCEPT THE NORTH AND SOUTH POLES

MISCHIEVOUS EYES

SHARP INCISORS, OFTEN YELLOWISH

BODY THAT RESEMBLES A GIANT MOUSE

WHISKERS (OR VIBRISSAE)

FEET WITH LITTLE CLAWS

TAIL THAT HELPS IT BALANCE

ORIGIN

Despite its bad reputation, the rat is an amazing rodent. Although rats are very smart and sociable, most people don't like rats, and that dislike goes back a very long time. During the Middle Ages, rats were blamed for spreading diseases like the black plague, but it turns out that the fleas living in the rats' fur were responsible. Since that time, most people have disliked rats.

- Rats make wonderful pets. They are playful and affectionate, and they really have a place in our homes. And, unlike mice, rats don't smell bad!

- Within a few weeks, your rat will adapt perfectly to its new home and look forward to exploring around the home. This is an opportunity for it to take the little objects that may be lying around and stash them in its favorite hiding place. If your things are disappearing, you'll know who to blame!

- Most rats are super-intelligent, have very good memories, and can easily learn tricks. Honestly, the rat is one of my very favorite pets.

- Be sure that your home is safe when you let your rat wander. A bottle of bleach, an open toilet bowl, a slamming door—all of these things are very dangerous for your rat.

MY OBSERVATIONS

Rats are great! I've had rats since the age of twelve, and I have wonderful memories of all of them. Unfortunately, rats only live to two to three years, which is not enough time to spend with these super companions.

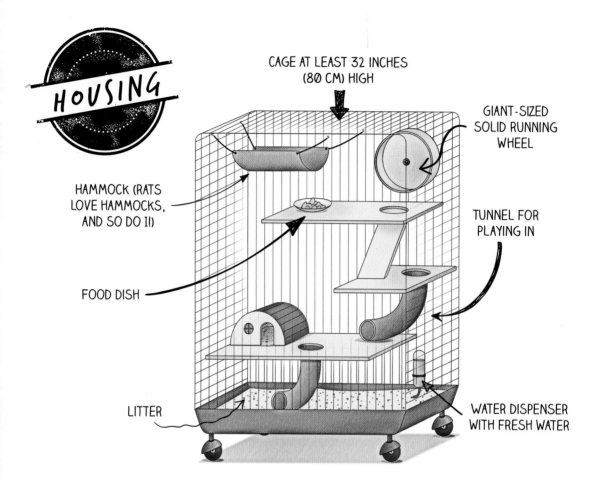

HOUSING

CAGE AT LEAST 32 INCHES (80 CM) HIGH

GIANT-SIZED SOLID RUNNING WHEEL

HAMMOCK (RATS LOVE HAMMOCKS, AND SO DO I!)

TUNNEL FOR PLAYING IN

FOOD DISH

LITTER

WATER DISPENSER WITH FRESH WATER

◆ Even though your rats' wild cousins can adapt to pretty much any living conditions, you still need to take good care of your rats. As I mentioned, rats are very sociable, and a rat left alone will get bored very quickly.

◆ Because rats can produce a lot of babies, I recommend that you adopt either two males or two females. If not, you will find yourself with a large family of rats! Choose young rats, as they will quickly learn to trust you.

◆ For their litter, choose hemp, coconut fiber, or flax. Do not use wood shavings. When rats urinate on wood shavings, the shavings give off a substance called *phenol*, which is harmful to the rats' lungs.

◆ Rats are nocturnal, meaning that they are awake at night, so putting the cage next to your bed may also keep you awake while they play at 3 o'clock in the morning!

◆ Get a large, solid exercise wheel with no bars, because the bars could easily break their tails.

◆ You can make a rat hammock out of an old T-shirt. Your rats will spend the day sleeping in it.

◆ Offer your rats small branches from fruit trees. They will love gnawing on them.

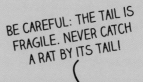

BE CAREFUL: THE TAIL IS FRAGILE. NEVER CATCH A RAT BY ITS TAIL!

CARE TIPS

Rats are clean animals that don't like to live in a dirty cage, so change the litter once a week and clean the entire cage thoroughly once a month with very hot water and a little white vinegar.

Your rats need to get out daily. Let them walk around in the evening while you're watching TV, and they will soon come to snuggle against your neck and be petted.

FEEDING

- Rats are omnivorous (they eat meat and plants) and greedy, so be careful not to give them rich food that will make them fat. A seed mixture made for rats, rat pellets, and a little high-quality dry dog or cat food make a good basic diet.

- You can offer your rats small pieces of fruit and some vegetables. Some rats like them; others not at all. Rats have individual tastes, just as we do.

- Keep the water dispenser full at all times. Give your rats fresh water every day along with their food.

GERBIL

Meriones unguiculatus

MONGOLIA

NOTE: ILLEGAL TO KEEP IN
CALIFORNIA AND HAWAII

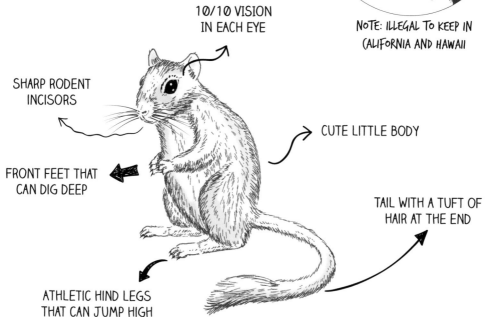

10/10 VISION
IN EACH EYE

SHARP RODENT
INCISORS

CUTE LITTLE BODY

FRONT FEET THAT
CAN DIG DEEP

TAIL WITH A TUFT OF
HAIR AT THE END

ATHLETIC HIND LEGS
THAT CAN JUMP HIGH

ORIGIN

This small rodent comes from Mongolia and northeastern China.
Gerbils are clever and adaptable and can survive a drought (a
very dry spell). They always live in a group and do not like being
alone. In the wild, they live in burrows (holes in the ground)
and are always looking out for predators when they go outside.

BEHAVIOR

- The first thing to remember is that gerbils need to live in a group. A gerbil living alone will be sad. You need at least two gerbils, and three is even better. Gerbils produce a lot of babies, so if you don't want to start raising a gerbil family, choose pets of the same sex.

- Gerbils love life! These small rodents from the deserts of Mongolia are usually healthy and full of energy.

- Their tails are covered with fur. People often like this better than the hairless tails of rats and mice.

- They are diurnal, meaning that they are awake and active during the day. They need a big cage for running, climbing, and playing.

- They may be shy at first, so be careful not to startle them when you handle them. Treat them gently. If you frighten a gerbil, it will use its teeth—and it will not be pleasant for you!

- Gerbils are not good pets for young children. They're too fast, and they are also quite fragile because they are small.

- Their tails can break easily, so never try to catch a gerbil by the tail.

MY OBSERVATIONS
Like most rodents, gerbils are sensitive to drafts and humidity. Keep this in mind when deciding where to set up their cage.

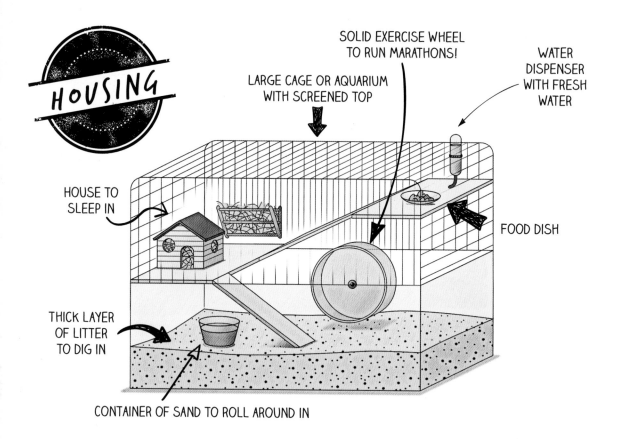

HOUSING

SOLID EXERCISE WHEEL TO RUN MARATHONS!

LARGE CAGE OR AQUARIUM WITH SCREENED TOP

WATER DISPENSER WITH FRESH WATER

HOUSE TO SLEEP IN

FOOD DISH

THICK LAYER OF LITTER TO DIG IN

CONTAINER OF SAND TO ROLL AROUND IN

♦ Gerbils need a large cage with different levels that they can explore all day long.

♦ Gerbils love to gnaw on everything, so make sure your cage is solid. If it isn't, they will escape. The same goes for anything inside the cage. Anything made out of wood will be gnawed to pieces.

♦ A thick layer of litter (hemp, coconut fiber, flax) is absolutely necessary so that the gerbils can dig as much as they want. They spend a lot of time digging, so choose a cage with a plastic bottom and high walls, or else they will send litter flying out of the cage in all directions.

♦ A large aquarium with a screened top is also a possibility. You will have to construct different levels to give them more space to explore.

♦ Fill a small house with hay. This will be their nest, where they will sleep at night.

♦ Gerbils spend a lot of time grooming their fur, and they love rolling in "bathing sand," a type of soft sand you can easily find at the pet-supply store. Set it up in a small container of sand inside the cage. The container will prevent them from spraying sand all over when they roll in it.

♦ Change the bathing sand and the litter once a week.

♦ An exercise wheel is an absolute must for your gerbils to let off steam and burn energy. Choose a solid wheel, because a wheel with bars can cause injuries if the gerbils get their legs or tails caught in the bars.

GERBIL

CARE TIPS

Gerbils are really fun to raise, but they need a lot of room in their cage. They hate being trapped in small spaces, so be sure to give these energetic pets a big home.

FEEDING

• Choose a high-quality seed mixture for gerbils that contains dried grasses and fruits. You can supplement this with a few dried insects, such as mealworms, which they will enjoy.

• Offer them plenty of hay, placed in a small hayrack, so they can chew it and keep their teeth from growing too long. In summer, you can also give them a little clover. They will love it.

• Gerbils are very curious and will come to eat treats, such as dried fruit, from your hand, which will help them quickly learn to trust you.

RUSSIAN DWARF HAMSTER

Phodopus sungorus

STEPPES OF CENTRAL ASIA

NOTE: ILLEGAL TO KEEP IN HAWAII

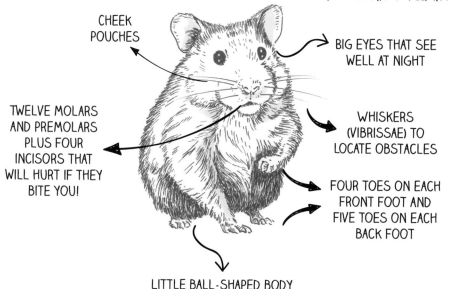

CHEEK POUCHES

BIG EYES THAT SEE WELL AT NIGHT

TWELVE MOLARS AND PREMOLARS PLUS FOUR INCISORS THAT WILL HURT IF THEY BITE YOU!

WHISKERS (VIBRISSAE) TO LOCATE OBSTACLES

FOUR TOES ON EACH FRONT FOOT AND FIVE TOES ON EACH BACK FOOT

LITTLE BALL-SHAPED BODY

ORIGIN

This charming little rodent comes from the deserts of central Asia. Where these hamsters live, the temperature can get very cold (as low as -4° Fahrenheit [−20° Celsius]). They live in burrows, where they make cozy nests using anything they can find on the surface, like dried grass. Living in the wild, they are mostly nocturnal (awake at night).

BEHAVIOR

- The Russian dwarf hamster is small but tough. It is also very energetic and needs a lot of space even though it is small.

- Your new hamster may be a little grumpy at first, and it will not like to be woken up when sleeping. Wait until it is awake and active before you handle it.

- This is a territorial animal that doesn't like sharing its space. You will need to raise your hamster alone, because more than one hamster will get into fights.

- Once your hamster trusts you, it will be a very sweet pet. It's also very curious, so once it wakes up in the evening, it will spend most of the night exploring its surroundings.

- Your hamster will be shy at first, and you will have to earn its trust. Offer treats, such as little bits of dried fruit, from your hand and pet it gently at the same time.

- Being very curious, your hamster will soon climb into your hand, and then you can carefully lift it out of its cage.

MY OBSERVATIONS

Your hamster may be so territorial that it will bite whatever enters its cage, fingers included. If that's what your hamster does, open the door of the cage and let it out before you try to handle it.

HOUSING

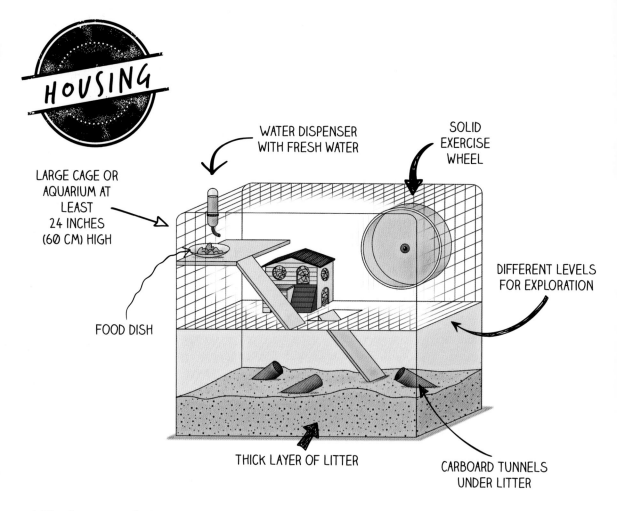

WATER DISPENSER
WITH FRESH WATER

SOLID
EXERCISE
WHEEL

LARGE CAGE OR
AQUARIUM AT
LEAST
24 INCHES
(60 CM) HIGH

DIFFERENT LEVELS
FOR EXPLORATION

FOOD DISH

THICK LAYER OF LITTER

CARBOARD TUNNELS
UNDER LITTER

◆ This hamster is little, but it needs space! You must give it a very large cage, or else it will soon feel trapped. It may even get upset and become aggressive. A cage measuring 24 x 16 inches (60 x 40 cm) is the minimum requirement. Choose a cage with different levels to give your hamster a bigger area for exploring.

◆ A thick layer of hemp or coconut fiber litter will be perfect. Make it 4 to 6 inches (10 to 15 cm) deep and then bury tunnels made from paper-towel tubes in the litter. It will love exploring these tunnels at night. A solid wheel will allow it to run off some energy.

◆ A small house with a sock or hay inside will serve as a cozy nest for it to sleep in during the day. Do not put cotton balls inside because they are dangerous if your hamster eats them.

◆ Think about where to place the cage. If you put it next to your bed, your hamster may keep you awake.

◆ Always handle your hamster on the floor or on a table. It's easy for the hamster to fall—unlike a cat, it will not always land on its feet!

RUSSIAN DWARF HAMSTER

FEEDING

- A mixture made for dwarf hamsters will be fine, even though this hamster tends to pick through its food and eat only what it likes best. To prevent this, you can buy pellets that contain all of the ingredients usually found in a mixture. Change its food dish every day.

- A little high-quality hay or dried grass will help wear down your hamster's teeth (which otherwise would just keep growing!).

- Dried insects added to its regular food provide some needed protein.

- A water dispenser filled with fresh water, changed daily, will keep your hamster properly hydrated.

A TINY TAIL!

STICK INSECT

Carausius morosus

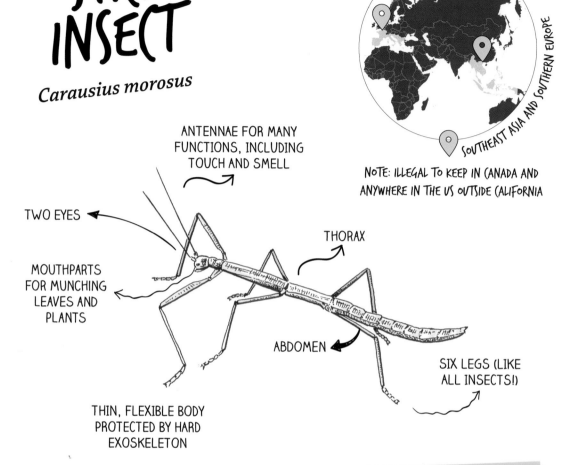

ANTENNAE FOR MANY FUNCTIONS, INCLUDING TOUCH AND SMELL

TWO EYES

MOUTHPARTS FOR MUNCHING LEAVES AND PLANTS

THORAX

ABDOMEN

SIX LEGS (LIKE ALL INSECTS!)

THIN, FLEXIBLE BODY PROTECTED BY HARD EXOSKELETON

SOUTHEAST ASIA AND SOUTHERN EUROPE

NOTE: ILLEGAL TO KEEP IN CANADA AND ANYWHERE IN THE US OUTSIDE CALIFORNIA

ORIGIN

There are more than 3,100 species of phasmid, but *Carausius morosus* is the name for the stick insect, also called a "walking stick." It is a master of camouflage: this creature blends in completely with its environment to look like a stick, making it difficult to spot. It can also fold up its legs against its body to be even less noticeable.

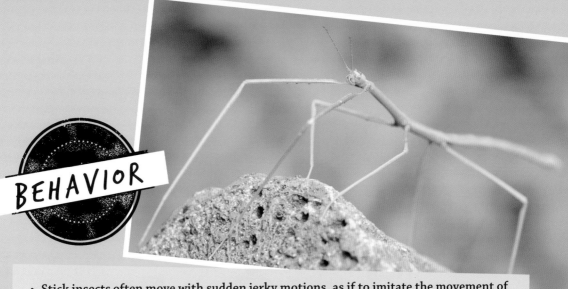

BEHAVIOR

- Stick insects often move with sudden jerky motions, as if to imitate the movement of tree branches in the wind.

- This insect measures about 4 inches (10 cm) in length and will molt (shed its skin) throughout its lifetime, seven times in all, from birth into adulthood.

- It is totally harmless and tends to be hunted when it lives in the wild. The stick insect has many predators (such as reptiles, birds, and spiders), but it doesn't eat other animals. It is 100 percent vegetarian.

- It is an easy animal to raise and can reproduce in large numbers in the right living conditions.

- Start with a group of young stick insects. You can watch them grow before they start producing babies. Normally, you will have both males and females in the group.

MY OBSERVATIONS

If you happen to have one or can find one, you can keep your stick insects in a French "cheese safe," which is a wooden-framed box with screened walls and shelves inside. This type of enclosure works very well and will keep your pets safely contained.

HOUSING

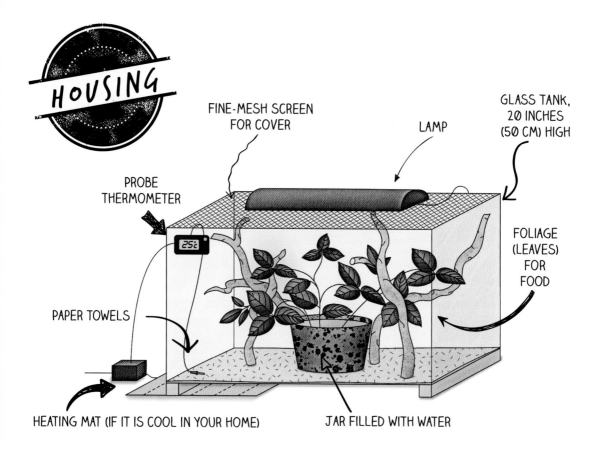

FINE-MESH SCREEN FOR COVER

LAMP

GLASS TANK, 20 INCHES (50 CM) HIGH

PROBE THERMOMETER

25℃

FOLIAGE (LEAVES) FOR FOOD

PAPER TOWELS

HEATING MAT (IF IT IS COOL IN YOUR HOME)

JAR FILLED WITH WATER

♦ Stick insects are easy to raise and good first pets for beginner insect-keepers. You can keep them in an aquarium or terrarium with a fine-mesh screen held in place with an elastic band. A tank measuring 20 inches (50 cm) high will do the job nicely.

♦ They like warmth: 77° Fahrenheit (25° Celsius) is the perfect temperature. Set up your tank near a radiator in the winter. If it ever gets too cold in your home, you can place a light bulb just outside the tank, on one side, or install a heating mat for reptiles.

♦ Place your tank in a bright area, near a window, but be careful about direct sunlight, which may raise the temperature in the tank too much.

♦ Lay paper towels on the bottom of the tank and change them regularly. You can use coconut fiber instead, but it will be very hard to find the eggs (which also happen to look like droppings!).

♦ In the middle of the tank, place a glass jar filled with water and a bouquet of your insects' favorite leaves.

♦ After a few months, when your stick insects are adults, the females will lay eggs regularly until the end of their lives, which is about six months later. A female can lay hundreds of eggs in her lifetime. It's interesting that, in some stick-insect species, females can lay eggs without even mating.

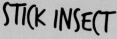

CARE TIPS

Stick-insect eggs are oval, brown, and tiny, measuring only a millimeter or two across. Place the eggs in a plastic box with a lid that has holes pierced in it for air. On the bottom of the box, lay paper towels that you keep damp, but not wet. If it is wet, the eggs will rot. Also, the eggs should not touch each other during incubation (the process of hatching in warm conditions). Place the box in a warm area (79° Fahrenheit [26° Celsius]) and wait patiently for two to three months, making sure to monitor the temperature. You should also keep the box slightly humid. The baby stick insects will measure less than half an inch (around 1 cm) at birth and can be raised in the same tank as the parents.

STICK INSECTS ARE CHAMPIONS OF CAMOUFLAGE. THESE LOOK LIKE LEAVES!

FEEDING

- The stick insect eats brambles (prickly shrubs and vines). It loves them—even if your fingers don't! You can easily find them in the woods.

- When you cut brambles, wear gardening gloves. Do not pick the ones at ground level, because animals may have urinated on them. Cut a big bunch of brambles to have extra on hand—when the stick insects have a family to feed, you'll see that they eat a lot! If you know that the brambles are clean, you can store them in the vegetable drawer of your refrigerator.

- Remove and replace the brambles in the tank if the leaves are dead. Be careful not to accidentally put any young stick insects in the trash at the same time!

- The stick insect also likes the leaves of privet hedges and rose bushes.

- Using a spray bottle, spray the foliage with water every morning. That's how your stick insects will get their drinking water.

AFRICAN PRAYING MANTIS

Sphodromantis lineola

CENTRAL AND WEST AFRICA

NOTE: NOTE: KEEPING THIS SPECIES IN THE US REQUIRES A USDA PERMIT AND APPROVED CONTAINMENT; ILLEGAL IN CANADA

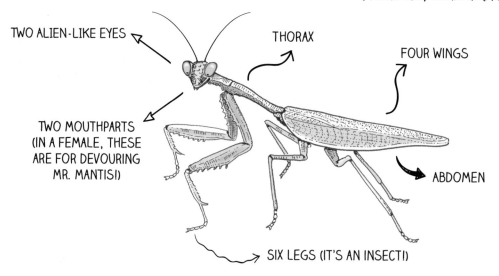

TWO ALIEN-LIKE EYES

THORAX

FOUR WINGS

TWO MOUTHPARTS (IN A FEMALE, THESE ARE FOR DEVOURING MR. MANTIS!)

ABDOMEN

SIX LEGS (IT'S AN INSECT!)

ORIGIN

Mantis religiosa is the praying mantis species that we see in the wild. It is a protected species in some regions. *Sphodromatis lineola*, the African praying mantis, is often bred in captivity and is common in the pet trade.

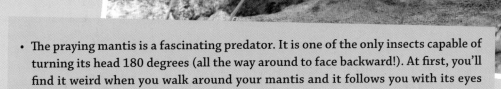

- The praying mantis is a fascinating predator. It is one of the only insects capable of turning its head 180 degrees (all the way around to face backward!). At first, you'll find it weird when you walk around your mantis and it follows you with its eyes without moving its body.

- The mantis has very good stereoscopic vision (depth perception), which helps it see its prey from a distance.

- The males are smaller than the females, which can grow up to 3 inches (8 cm) long. Both sexes can fly, although the females fly a lot less because they weigh more.

- The front legs are impressive weapons. Equipped with spines, they spear the prey and hold it in place while the mantis eats. The mantis also uses these legs to defend itself.

- The female praying mantis is known for eating the male during mating, and this is no urban legend!

MY OBSERVATIONS

There are many species of mantis available, but the African praying mantis is the most common. It's easy to find in specialty stores at an affordable price.

THIS *IDOLOMANTIS DIABOLICA* ("DEVIL'S FLOWER MANTIS") IS REALLY SUPERB LOOKING!

HOUSING

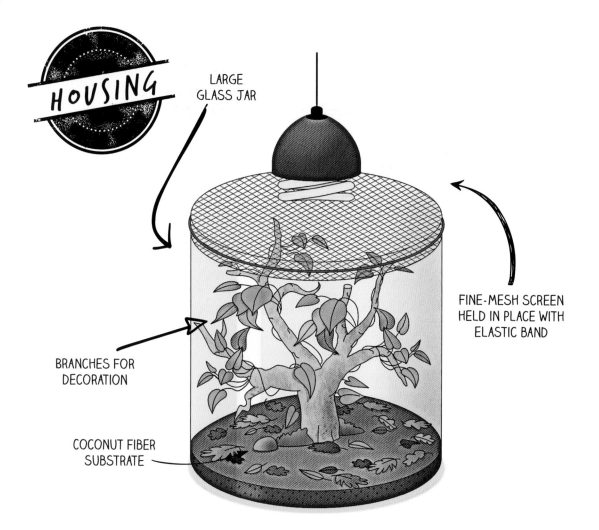

LARGE GLASS JAR

FINE-MESH SCREEN HELD IN PLACE WITH ELASTIC BAND

BRANCHES FOR DECORATION

COCONUT FIBER SUBSTRATE

◆ You can keep your mantis in one of several types of container, such as a large glass jar, a tall plastic box, or a small terrarium. Whatever you choose, use fine-mesh screen to cover the top. This species is tree-dwelling, so make sure that its home is at least 8 inches (20 cm) high.

◆ At the bottom, add coconut fiber substrate and keep it damp. Add branches for decoration and for your praying mantis to hang onto, even if it mostly likes to hang upside down from the screen at the top of the container.

◆ Mantises molt (shed their skin) regularly as they grow, and this is fascinating to watch.

◆ Keep only one mantis per container. Otherwise, they may eat each other.

◆ Lightly spray the habitat with water several times a week for your mantis to drink and to maintain the right level of humidity. A temperature of 73 to 77° Fahrenheit (23 to 25° Celsius) will be perfect.

➧ You can handle your praying mantis gently but be careful not to drop it!

➧ If you have a female and you find a male, you can try to mate them, but you need to be careful. Feed your female plenty so that the male doesn't become her meal even before they mate. And prepare to say goodbye to your male afterward. Males rarely survive mating.

➧ A few weeks after mating, the female will lay an ootheca (sort of an "egg case" full of eggs) that she will attach to a wall or branch in her habitat. A few weeks after that, dozens of young mantises only a few millimeters long will come out of the ootheca. Quickly isolate them, one by one, in containers with lids. Otherwise, they will soon eat each other. You can feed them drosophilas (small fruit flies).

FEEDING

• Mantises are always hungry! Your mantis will eat just about any insect you offer it—grasshoppers in summer, flies, crickets, worms—they're not picky eaters.

• To give your mantis drinking water, you only need to spray water inside the habitat regularly.

REGAL JUMPING SPIDER

Phidippus regius

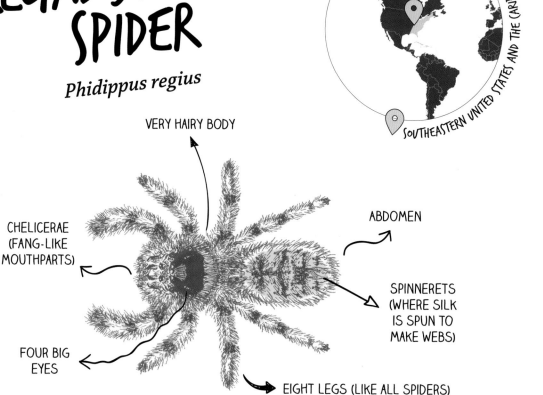

VERY HAIRY BODY

CHELICERAE (FANG-LIKE MOUTHPARTS)

FOUR BIG EYES

ABDOMEN

SPINNERETS (WHERE SILK IS SPUN TO MAKE WEBS)

EIGHT LEGS (LIKE ALL SPIDERS)

SOUTHEASTERN UNITED STATES AND THE CARIBBEAN

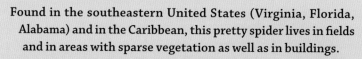

ORIGIN

Found in the southeastern United States (Virginia, Florida, Alabama) and in the Caribbean, this pretty spider lives in fields and in areas with sparse vegetation as well as in buildings.

Scientists from the University of Manchester in England have studied its uncommon jumping abilities. It propels itself with so much force that it can leap a distance six times the length of its own body! Scientists do not yet understand the secret of this jumping power, but it is a mechanism that could someday be used in the design of a robot.

BEHAVIOR

This spider is very cute, with its big eyes set at the front of its head!

- It is able to jump to get around and to catch its prey, which it will bring back to its web.

- It is small, with the females measuring only a little more than half an inch (about 1.5 cm) in length. The males are smaller.

- Female jumping spiders come in interesting colors that differ according to where they come from. Males don't have the same colors. They are black and white with areas of reflective metallic green.

- You can try to handle your spider gently, but be careful. If you frighten it, it will jump to avoid danger, so always keep an eye on it.

- This species is totally harmless—to you, but not to its prey!

CAUGHT IN MID-FLIGHT!

MY OBSERVATIONS

Spiders are truly fascinating to observe, whether they are hunting or shedding their skin. This species is perfect for a beginner. You can even start a spider family if you are lucky enough to find a couple.

HOUSING

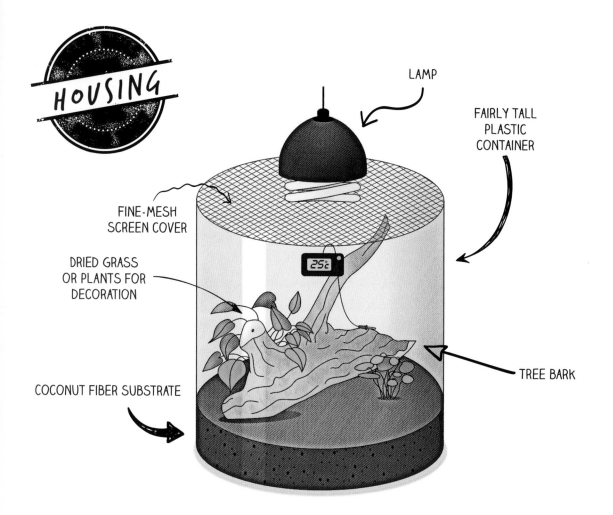

LAMP

FAIRLY TALL PLASTIC CONTAINER

FINE-MESH SCREEN COVER

DRIED GRASS OR PLANTS FOR DECORATION

25℃

TREE BARK

COCONUT FIBER SUBSTRATE

◆ The jumping spider can be kept in many different types of container, from a simple plastic box to a small terrarium. Even a vase can do the job. The important thing is to have a container that is tall enough and wide enough to allow it to move comfortably. A fine-mesh screen for a cover will provide adequate airflow.

◆ At the bottom, lay a substrate of coconut fiber that you will keep slightly damp. Add a piece of tree bark on which the spider will weave its web. The web is not necessarily a trap for insects, but more of a shelter for the spider.

◆ You can add a few plants to decorate the enclosure. The spider will walk on the leaves to hunt its favorite prey.

◆ The ideal temperature is 77° Fahrenheit (25° Celsius) to raise this species.

CARE TIPS

Caution! If your spider refuses to eat one day, it may be because it is preparing to molt (shed its skin). In this case, remove the prey from the enclosure, because it may attack the spider during this time when the spider is unprotected. Wait a few days after it has molted and then offer it the prey.

FEEDING

- This spider is an impressive hunter that can attack many kinds of prey, even prey that is larger than it is. You can offer it grasshoppers, small crickets, or "red runner" cockroaches.

- Feed your spider twice a week.

- You can hydrate it by lightly spraying its habitat with water twice a week.

CRANWELL'S HORNED FROG

Ceratophrys cranwelli

ARGENTINA, BRAZIL, PARAGUAY

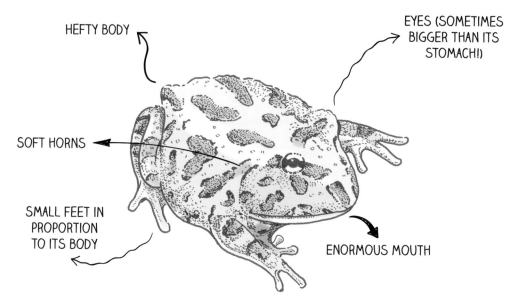

HEFTY BODY

EYES (SOMETIMES BIGGER THAN ITS STOMACH!)

SOFT HORNS

SMALL FEET IN PROPORTION TO ITS BODY

ENORMOUS MOUTH

ORIGIN

In its natural habitat in South America, this wonderful frog is active at night. It is a land frog that uses its powerful legs to burrow underground during the dry season.

I would describe this species of amphibian as a glutton (greedy when it comes to food). It eats everything it can, even larger prey. This pretty frog can be found in captivity in many different colors, with the albino form being the most common.

BEHAVIOR

- This 100 percent land species hunts from a blind, meaning that it digs a hole and waits patiently for prey to pass within its reach. It can stay totally still for hours and then suddenly jump on its prey and gobble it up.

- Its appetite is so big that it's also called the "Pac-Man frog." Do not overfeed it, because obesity will shorten its life.

- This frog doesn't really like being handled.

- The males are smaller than the females (4 inches [10 cm] versus 6 inches [15 cm] for the females). Males sing once they become adults (between eight months and one year old), which could be a problem if you want a quiet night. It's impossible to know the sex of this frog when it's young, so you will have to wait and see!

- These frogs live six to ten years in captivity.

MY OBSERVATIONS

You can start by raising your *Ceratophrys* in a small tank for the first few months and then increase the size of the frog's home as it grows.

HOUSING

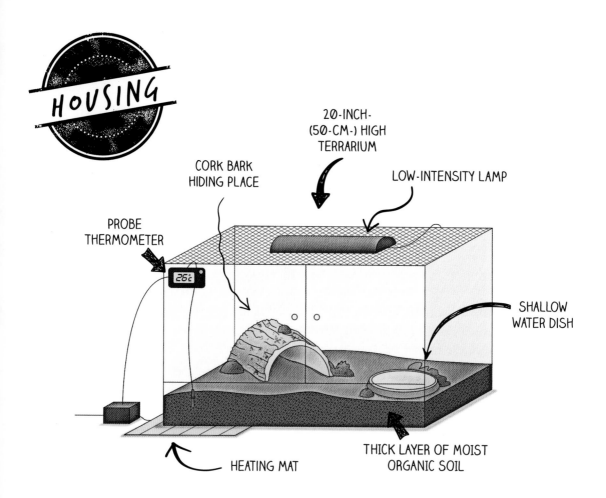

20-INCH- (50-CM-) HIGH TERRARIUM

LOW-INTENSITY LAMP

CORK BARK HIDING PLACE

PROBE THERMOMETER

26℃

SHALLOW WATER DISH

HEATING MAT

THICK LAYER OF MOIST ORGANIC SOIL

◆ It's very easy to raise this frog in a terrarium. Keep only one per tank. If there are two, one will eat the other as soon as it gets hungry!

◆ It will need a thick layer of substrate, about 4 inches (10 cm) deep, in which it will dig holes and spend most of its time. Organic soil without fertilizer, a humus mixture of coconut fiber and ground sphagnum moss, or a combination of both will work well. The substrate must be wet.

◆ A shallow water dish will allow it to bathe from time to time, and some cork bark will provide a hiding place.

◆ For this tropical species, 77 to 79° Fahrenheit (25 to 26° Celsius) is ideal. To maintain this temperature, use a small reptile heating mat on one side of the terrarium. Use a heating mat with a thermostat so you can easily control the temperature.

◆ If you add lighting, do not make it too intense. This frog doesn't like bright light.

◆ You can grow plants, such as pothos, in your tank, which will help make the environment more natural.

FEEDING

- When you buy your frog, it is usually very small, about the size of a quarter, but if you feed it properly, it will quickly grow to about 6 inches (15 cm) in length in less than two years.

- Start by feeding it crickets appropriate to its size. Offer it increasingly larger prey as it grows.

- After a few months, you can offer thawed rodents, which you will dangle in front of your frog's nose with tweezers. Your frog will pounce on them. You must not feed your frog live rodents. It's not nice for the mice, and it's dangerous for the frog if a mouse bites it.

- Feed your frog twice a week if you give it insects, and once every ten days if you give it rodents, which are much higher in protein. It will also enjoy fish.

AFRICAN BULLFROG

Pyxicephalus adspersus

SOUTH AFRICA AND EAST AFRICA

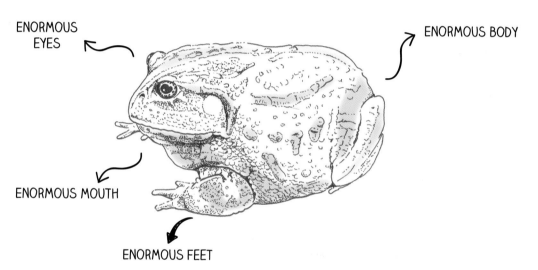

ENORMOUS EYES

ENORMOUS BODY

ENORMOUS MOUTH

ENORMOUS FEET

ORIGIN

This frog is native to South Africa and East Africa. It is especially resistant to drought (dry conditions).

It spends most of the year underground, patiently waiting for the rainy season, when it will have only a few months to fill up on food, mate, and give birth to hundreds of tadpoles (larvae).

- This species is simply *enormous* as an adult. It's one of the largest amphibians in the world. The males are much larger than the females, and some males can reach a truly impressive size.

- The bullfrog is very calm and often stays still. It does, however, have amazingly fast eating reflexes, leaving little chance of escape for anything that comes close to its huge mouth.

- This nocturnal giant will grow from just 1/10 ounce (a few grams) when you buy it to almost 5 pounds (more than 1 kg) in a few years. It is greedy and will bite anything within reach of its mouth, including your fingers.

- If you add plants to your tank, this bulldozer of a frog may squash them in no time.

- Like snakes, frogs molt (shed their skin) regularly, and they often eat what they shed. If one morning you see your frog with totally new skin in shimmering colors, it's because it molted during the night.

- Adult males may begin to sing. They are not too loud, but if you keep the terrarium in your bedroom, the singing might keep you up at night. As with the horned frog, it is impossible to know the sex of a young frog when you buy it, so you may get a surprise once it reaches adult size!

MY OBSERVATIONS

Increase the size of your frog's home as it grows. Avoid handling it too much. Amphibians in general do not like being handled.

USE TWEEZERS TO FEED YOUR BULLFROG.

HOUSING

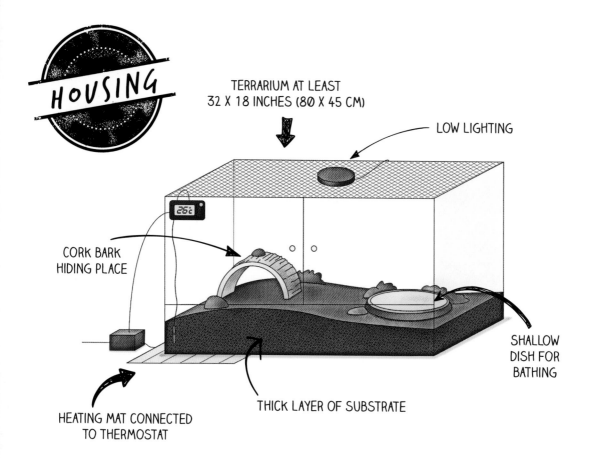

TERRARIUM AT LEAST
32 X 18 INCHES (80 X 45 CM)

LOW LIGHTING

CORK BARK
HIDING PLACE

SHALLOW
DISH FOR
BATHING

HEATING MAT CONNECTED
TO THERMOSTAT

THICK LAYER OF SUBSTRATE

◆ In captivity, this frog requires a damp environment all year round. At the bottom of the terrarium, place a thick layer of substrate (a mixture of organic soil without fertilizer, coconut fiber, and ground sphaghum moss at least 4 inches [10 cm] deep). Moisten the substrate regularly with lukewarm water.

◆ Maintain a temperature of 79 to 81° Fahrenheit (26 to 27° Celsius) during the day and a few degrees lower at night, using a heating mat for reptiles connected to a thermostat.

◆ Low lighting for ten hours per day will recreate a day/night cycle.

◆ A shallow bowl will serve as your frog's bathtub and often its toilet as well, so clean it thoroughly and change the water several times a week.

CARE TIPS

Deep-cleaning the water dish and changing the water several times a week is absolutely necessary. Your house-cleaning better get five-star reviews!

FEEDING

- Feed your frog in proportion to its size: a few adult crickets every three days at the start, and then cockroaches and thawed rodents. The larger the prey, the less frequently you feed the frog.

- Once the frog reaches adulthood, one small thawed rat every ten days will be plenty.

- You can also offer it thawed baby chicks. Just like when feeding it a rodent, dangle the prey in front of your frog with tweezers, and it will leap to catch the prey.

- Overfeeding is not good for your frog. It may grow more quickly, but it will have a shorter life span, which can be more than ten years. Remember: in nature, prey can be hard to find, and animals eat less than they would in captivity, so don't let your frog become obese.

WOODLOUSE

Order Isopoda

NOTE: MAY REQUIRE USDA PERMIT TO KEEP AND
TRANSPORT, DEPENDING ON SPECIES AND SOURCE

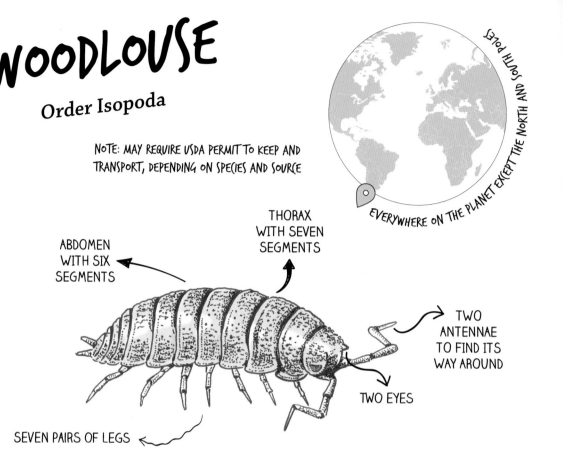

EVERYWHERE ON THE PLANET EXCEPT THE NORTH AND SOUTH POLES

ABDOMEN
WITH SIX
SEGMENTS

THORAX
WITH SEVEN
SEGMENTS

TWO
ANTENNAE
TO FIND ITS
WAY AROUND

TWO EYES

SEVEN PAIRS OF LEGS

ORIGIN

• The mere thought of lice is unpleasant, but woodlice are actually quite charming little creatures. In some regions, they have different nicknames, such as "roly-polies" or "pill bugs." They are found just about everywhere in the world where there is decomposing wood.

• These animals are not insects but crustaceans, from the same family as shrimp, although I wouldn't suggest eating them!

• There are more than 3,000 species of woodlouse. What makes them special is their rigid exoskeleton (outer shell) that they shed during the molting phase.

BEHAVIOR

- These detrivores, or decomposers, take care of transforming dead wood into organic matter that feeds trees and plants.

- They live in colonies and are very useful creatures, working almost unnoticeably.

- They have the interesting ability to roll up into balls, just like marbles, when they sense danger. But we don't play marbles with woodlice!

- It's very easy to raise woodlice. To find them, head outdoors with a jar and lift up pieces of old trees that are rotting on the ground. You'll see groups of these little animals. You don't need to collect too many. A dozen will be plenty for you to start breeding.

MY OBSERVATIONS

Breeding woodlice is fun and educational, and it costs nothing. Woodlice are really interesting to observe. Being easy to raise, they are the perfect candidates for beginners. They are a good way for children to practice taking care of animals.

HOUSING

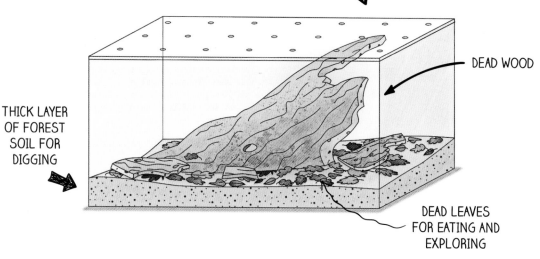

PLASTIC BOX
WITH AIR HOLES

DEAD WOOD

THICK LAYER
OF FOREST
SOIL FOR
DIGGING

DEAD LEAVES
FOR EATING AND
EXPLORING

◆ In a plastic box or a small terrarium, lay a thick layer of forest soil along with crushed dead leaves.

◆ Ensure proper ventilation by piercing the cover with tiny holes. Make sure the holes are not too big, or the woodlice will escape.

◆ Spray the substrate with water to make it damp but not soaking wet.

◆ Add pieces of rotting wood from the forest, and your woodlouse home is ready. You can now release the woodlice into their new habitat.

◆ Room temperature is fine for them. There's no need for special lighting; they don't like bright light.

◆ You will soon see young woodlice that are miniature versions of their parents. When you find that many babies have been born, you can release them back into the woods where you first found their parents.

CARE TIPS

Make sure to keep their habitat clean. Replace their food regularly to avoid mold, which they do not like.

FEEDING

- Place a slice of zucchini or a piece of ripe fruit in a small dish. They will really love it.

LAND HERMIT CRAB

Coenobita sp.

FROM EAST AFRICA TO THE PACIFIC OCEAN, CARIBBEAN, BERMUDA, FLORIDA

NOTE: ILLEGAL TO KEEP IN HAWAII

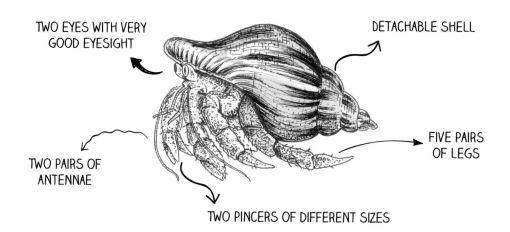

TWO EYES WITH VERY
GOOD EYESIGHT

DETACHABLE SHELL

TWO PAIRS OF
ANTENNAE

FIVE PAIRS
OF LEGS

TWO PINCERS OF DIFFERENT SIZES

ORIGIN

There are many species of land hermit crabs. They live in large groups on beaches, where they walk on the ground and climb on plants in search of food.

Land hermit crabs have become very popular, and it's no wonder. They are complex and amazing animals. Unfortunately, they are victims of their own popularity. These animals are more often viewed as toys than as living pets.

The kits sold in many souvenir shops for keeping land hermit crabs are truly awful—usually a simple plastic aquarium and shells painted the colors of comic-book characters. To keep hermit crabs this way means certain death for them, and you must not do this!

BEHAVIOR

- They are very friendly and social. You must be prepared to adopt at least five or six or them and care for them properly.

- They change shells regularly as they grow, taking over empty shells that other crabs have left behind.

- They need seawater to reproduce. The larvae grow in the water, but apart from this stage, the hermit crabs live on land (and sometimes in trees!).

- They can easily be raised in captivity with the proper housing and care.

- It is fascinating to watch them interacting with each other.

MY OBSERVATIONS
When your hermit crabs burrow underground, it's because they are going to molt (shed the exoskeleton). Do not uncover them! Be patient, and you will soon see them come out brand new.

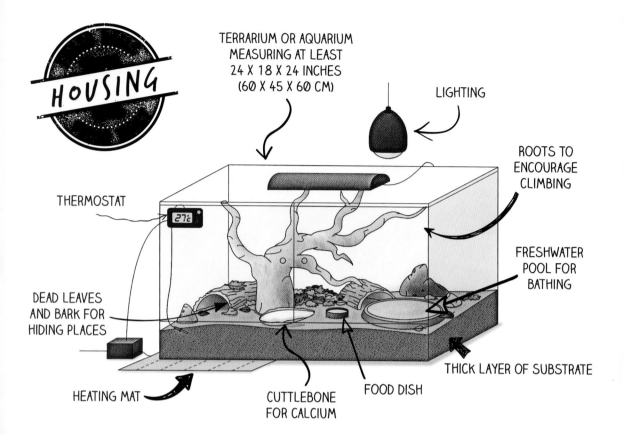

HOUSING

TERRARIUM OR AQUARIUM MEASURING AT LEAST 24 X 18 X 24 INCHES (60 X 45 X 60 CM)

LIGHTING

ROOTS TO ENCOURAGE CLIMBING

THERMOSTAT

FRESHWATER POOL FOR BATHING

DEAD LEAVES AND BARK FOR HIDING PLACES

THICK LAYER OF SUBSTRATE

HEATING MAT

CUTTLEBONE FOR CALCIUM

FOOD DISH

◆ You must have the right equipment for your hermit crabs' care and well-being! You will need to spend money on the proper housing and equipment, but that's the price you need to pay to properly raise these animals, which can live for more than ten years.

◆ An aquarium or terrarium of at least 24 x 18 x 24 inches (60 x 45 x 60 cm) is a must. A large section of the cover should be glass or plexiglass to maintain the high humidity they are used to in their tropical homes in the wild.

◆ On the bottom you will need a thick layer of substrate, at least 5 inches (12 cm) deep, made of 60 percent sandbox sand and 40 percent coconut fiber humus. Keep the substrate damp by regularly spraying it with water.

◆ Sturdy aquarium roots, set well into the substrate, allow the crabs to climb.

◆ A shallow pool of fresh water is essential for them to bathe in. Change the water daily.

◆ In one corner of the tank, make hiding places for them out of a little pile of leaves and some upside-down pieces of cork bark.

◆ Place a heating mat for reptiles, connected to a thermostat, under half of the tank. A temperature of 79 to 82° Fahrenheit (26 to 28° Celsius) is necessary for the crabs' well-being.

◆ Lighting connected to a timer will recreate a day/night cycle.

◆ Place their food in a small dish and offer them a cuttlebone to give them the calcium they need to grow. Change their food daily.

◆ Spray the habitat regularly with lukewarm water that has sat out for twenty-four hours (to allow any chlorine to evaporate). The humidity is important for them.

◆ My personal advice is to add UV lights to the tank. They are sold in pet-supply stores. UV rays are blocked by glass, so place the lighting above the screened area or inside the tank.

◆ Be creative and make the tank look really nice!

CARE TIPS
Give them new empty shells regularly. You can buy them in specialty pet-supply stores or online. The shapes of decorative painted shells are rarely suitable, so buy natural shells.

FEEDING

• These animals are omnivores; they eat animal- and plant-based foods, such as fruit, vegetables, dried insects, and pellets for aquarium crabs as well as eggshells, walnuts, tofu, seeds, fish, and more.

• Because they will try just about anything, offer them many different foods. Have fun and vary the menu (chocolate, however, is not a good idea!).

• Be sure to thoroughly rinse fruits and vegetables to remove any chemicals. Organic produce is better for them, as it is for us.

WESTERN MOSQUITOFISH

Gambusia affinis

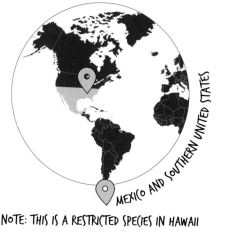

MEXICO AND SOUTHERN UNITED STATES

NOTE: THIS IS A RESTRICTED SPECIES IN HAWAII

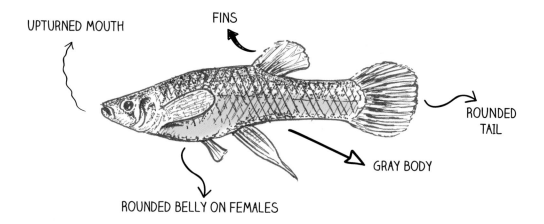

UPTURNED MOUTH

FINS

ROUNDED TAIL

GRAY BODY

ROUNDED BELLY ON FEMALES

ORIGIN

The Western mosquitofish is a very hardy fish that eats mosquito larvae in regions where there are a lot of mosquitoes.

Mosquitofish are native to Mexico and the southern United States, but they have been introduced to many other parts of the world to help eradicate mosquitoes. For example, they can now be found in France, in the Camargue, where there is plenty of work for them! They are currently being studied for their impact on the environment and especially on local fish populations.

BEHAVIOR

- The mosquitofish is in the same family as the guppy but is less colorful and a lot hardier. It adapts easily to different temperatures and different water qualities.

- Mosquitofish are easy to care for, so they are ideal for beginning aquarium enthusiasts.

- If all goes well, you will soon find baby mosquitofish that were born in your aquarium. They will appear on the water's surface and will grow quickly.

MY OBSERVATIONS

Place your aquarium in a dimly lit area of a room. Direct sun from a window can raise the temperature too high and cause algae to form.

HOUSING

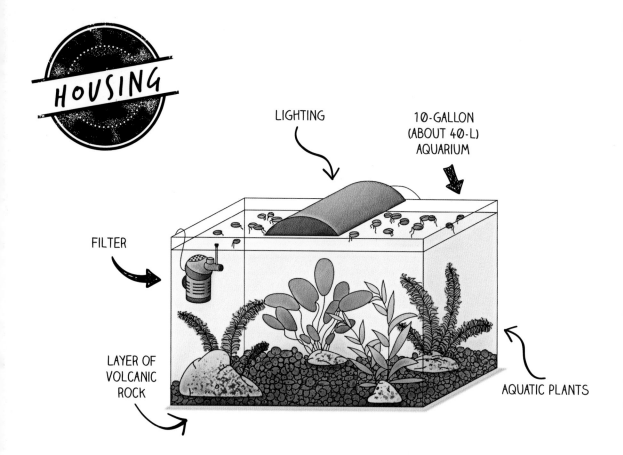

LIGHTING

10-GALLON (ABOUT 40-L) AQUARIUM

FILTER

LAYER OF VOLCANIC ROCK

AQUATIC PLANTS

◆ The first thing you need when keeping fish is patience. You must set up the aquarium and then wait a month before getting your first fish. If you add fish too soon, things won't work out well. There's a simple reason: waiting a month allows enough time for the right bacteria to grow, and this bacteria will consume your fishes' waste and help keep the water healthy. If you set up your tank and put the fish in right away, the water will quickly become dirty and polluted—and toxic for your fish! So follow my advice and be patient.

◆ A 10-gallon (40-L) aquarium will be perfect for starting out with mosquitofish. At the bottom of the aquarium, spread about a 1-inch (2- to 3-cm) layer of pozzolana, a volcanic gravel that you can easily find at a garden store. Rinse it thoroughly beforehand,

because it is often full of dust, which is not good if you want clear water. This gravel makes a very good home for bacteria and will increase your aquarium's natural filtration.

◆ Fill a bucket with tap water and allow it to sit for twenty-four hours to allow any chlorine in the water to evaporate. Use this water to fill your tank slowly and carefully.

◆ It's time for the gardening stage! Cabomba and waterweed are good candidates. They are sturdy and attractive aquatic plants. They will also serve as hiding places for baby mosquitofish when they are born.

◆ Put a small filter in the tank. These are easy to find and are not expensive. Place the filter against one of the tank walls, about an inch (2 to 3 cm) from the surface. Direct the outtake toward the surface to ensure that the water is properly oxygenated.

♦ Install aquarium lighting that will help the plants grow and will create a day/night cycle for the fish. Connect the lighting to a small mechanical timer and set it for eight hours of light per day at first, to help limit the growth of algae. After a few weeks, gradually increase the lighting to ten hours per day.

♦ All that's left to do is wait one month, and then you can put your first fish in the tank!

♦ Start with more females than males. One male and three females will be perfect.

♦ The day your fish arrive, let their bag soak for at least fifteen minutes in the tank to balance the water temperatures. Then slowly pour a little water from the tank into the bag. After twenty minutes, release your fish into their new home.

CARE TIPS
Every two weeks, replace about 20 percent of the aquarium water with new settled water. At this time, also clean the filter in the water that you are discarding from the tank. Warning: If you clean the filter under running water from the tap, you will kill all of the good bacteria in the filter.

FEEDING

• Your fish should be fed twice a day, once in the morning and once in the late afternoon, in small quantities.

• Exotic-fish flakes are very good for this species. The fish must eat them right away; do not allow leftover flakes to stay in the water.

• If you see flakes in the water after your fish have finished eating, it means you have fed them too much, and you will have a problem with dirty water. Adjust the amount of food so that they immediately eat everything you give them.

SIAMESE FIGHTING FISH (BETTA)

Betta splendens

SOUTHEAST ASIA

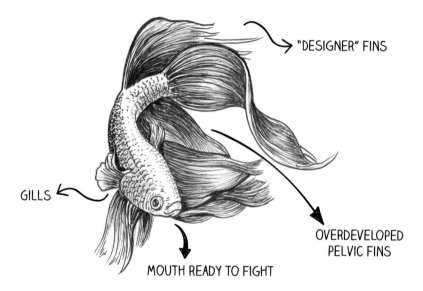

"DESIGNER" FINS

GILLS

OVERDEVELOPED PELVIC FINS

MOUTH READY TO FIGHT

ORIGIN

The Siamese fighting fish, or betta, is very popular with aquarium lovers. It has been raised for hundreds of years in its native country, Thailand. People have bred betta fish with incredible colors and beautiful fins, so our pet bettas look very different from their wild relatives.

The name "Siamese fighting fish" comes from the fact that the males fight each other. In Thailand, people even place bets on these fish fights!

BEHAVIOR

SOME TYPES OF
SIAMESE FIGHTING FISH
HAVE SMALL FINS.

- In the wild, this fish lives in the shallow waters of rice paddies (fields), which are low-oxygen environments.

- Unlike other fish, the betta does not draw oxygen from the water but breathes on the surface using its "labyrinth," a special breathing organ.

- During the reproduction period, the male will make a nest of bubbles on the water's surface and will protect the eggs while they develop.

WARNING!
Cover your tank. Fighting fish have a tendency to leap high, and you don't want to risk finding your fish on the floor.

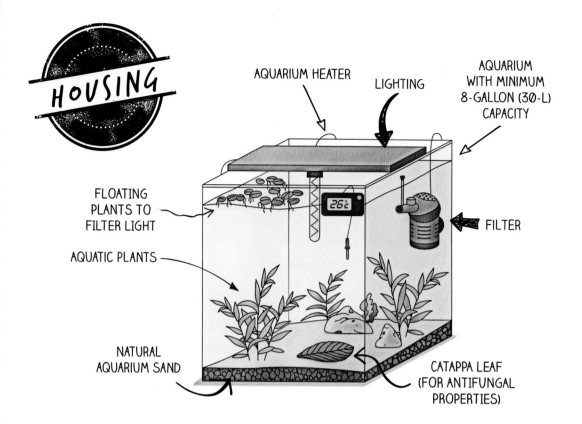

HOUSING

AQUARIUM HEATER

LIGHTING

AQUARIUM WITH MINIMUM 8-GALLON (30-L) CAPACITY

FLOATING PLANTS TO FILTER LIGHT

AQUATIC PLANTS

FILTER

26°c

NATURAL AQUARIUM SAND

CATAPPA LEAF (FOR ANTIFUNGAL PROPERTIES)

◆ Too often sold in a glass of water, without proper advice, this magnificent fish is often cared for poorly. It deserves a lot better, including a proper aquarium and the necessary equipment for its well-being.

◆ To keep your fish happy and healthy for its three-year life span, keep it alone in an 8-gallon (30-L) aquarium.

◆ Lay a thick layer of thoroughly rinsed natural aquarium sand or volcanic rock at the bottom of the tank. This will allow the plants to be properly rooted. Add a few fertilizer balls for aquatic plants, and the plants will thrive. Add enough plants to make the environment look as natural as possible.

◆ Aquarium lighting giving ten hours of light per day will be perfect for helping your plants grow. Your fighting fish doesn't like bright light, so add plants on the surface to filter the light.

◆ You can fill your tank with tap water, but let it sit for twenty-four hours first to give the chlorine time to evaporate. A small filter will help you get proper water quality, and a heating system (1 watt per liter of water) will help ensure a temperature of 79° Fahrenheit (26° Celsius).

◆ Once the tank is fully set up with plants, water, and accessories, let it run for one month before introducing your fish. This will establish the proper nitrogen cycle and water balance.

SIAMESE FIGHTING FISH (BETTA)

➤ On the day you bring your betta home, soak the bag containing the fish for at least fifteen minutes in the tank to get it used to the water temperature. Then, gradually add water from the tank into the bag. Finally, after twenty minutes, release the fish into its new home. Now you can begin admiring it!

FEEDING

- Pellets made for fighting fish along with some thawed mudworms make a good basic diet.

- Make sure your fish eats everything within a few minutes; uneaten food will pollute the water. Feed it several times a day, but in tiny quantities.

CARE TIPS
Keep a catappa (Indian almond) leaf in the aquarium permanently. This leaf, from a tree that grows in tropical regions, is easy to find in stores. It has antifungal properties that will protect your betta's fins.

THIS FIGHTING FISH HAS LARGE FINS.

BUDGETT'S FROG

Lepidobatrachus laevis

PARAGUAY, URUGUAY, AND ARGENTINA

EYES TURNED UPWARD

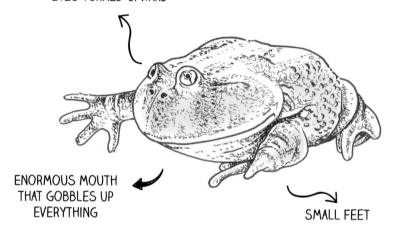

ENORMOUS MOUTH THAT GOBBLES UP EVERYTHING

SMALL FEET

ORIGIN

Budgett's frog lives in shallow swamps in South America. When the swamps dry up, it burrows underground for several months, waiting for winter and the rainy season.

This frog can defend itself. Its lower jaw is equipped with two teeth. Its body swells up when it is attacked, and it can scream to frighten off predators!

BEHAVIOR

- This species may not be the prettiest, but it is endearing. A real stomach on legs, it will swallow anything moving in front of it, even its fellow frogs!

- This hardy frog has a particular look that people either love or hate.

- Its adult size is about 4 inches (10 cm), so it's more manageable than an African bullfrog, which needs more space, but it has the same enormous appetite.

- In captivity, this species is basically 100 percent aquatic, meaning that it lives only in the water. It can live about ten years in captivity.

- These animals do not enjoy being handled, so try to avoid it.

MY OBSERVATIONS
Keep only one frog, because cannibalism (eating each other) occurs frequently in this species (1 + 1 = 1!).

HOUSING

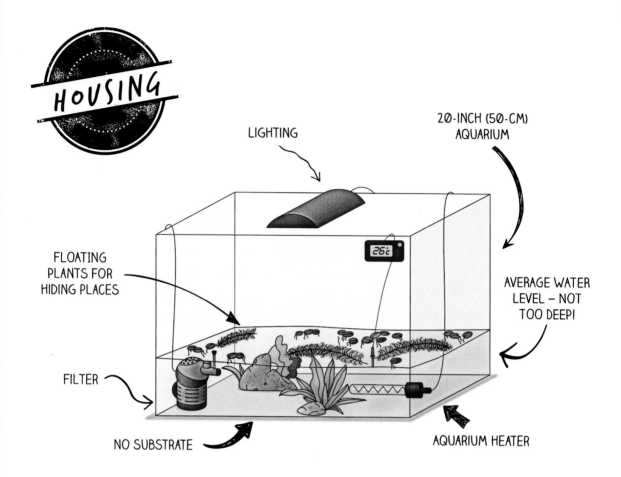

LIGHTING

20-INCH (50-CM) AQUARIUM

FLOATING PLANTS FOR HIDING PLACES

AVERAGE WATER LEVEL – NOT TOO DEEP!

FILTER

NO SUBSTRATE

AQUARIUM HEATER

◆ An aquarium is a must. Although this species rarely leaves the water, you need to be careful. If the water is too deep, your frog could drown! A water level of about 4 inches (10 cm) will be perfect.

◆ Before filling the aquarium, let the water sit for twenty-four hours in a bucket to allow the chlorine to evaporate.

◆ The frog will thrive in an aquarium 20 cm (50 cm) high, with water heated to 79 to 81° Fahrenheit (26 to 27° Celsius) by a small aquarium heater.

◆ Don't put any substrate at the bottom of the aquarium. The frog could easily ingest sand, which could get impacted (stuck) inside his body. Sand may also scratch the frog, whose skin is very fragile.

◆ A small filter in the tank will keep your water clear and clean. Important: You must clean the sponge inside the filter every week.

◆ You can add some floating plants for decoration, and your frog will also use them as hiding places. Lighting set to ten hours per day on a timer will allow your plants to grow properly.

ISN'T IT JUST ADORABLE?

CARE TIPS

Because this frog eats a lot, it will also dirty the tank water a lot, so change about half the water in the tank once a week. Alternatively, you could get a larger filter, but be careful not to create too much of a current in the tank, because the frog won't like it. If necessary, direct the water flow of the filter toward one of the tank walls to weaken the current.

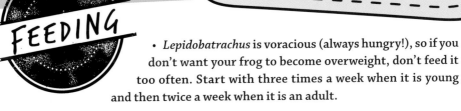

FEEDING

- *Lepidobatrachus* is voracious (always hungry!), so if you don't want your frog to become overweight, don't feed it too often. Start with three times a week when it is young and then twice a week when it is an adult.

- On the menu: crickets, earthworms, pellets for axolotls (Mexican walking fish), small thawed fish…your frog will eat them all!

- You can occasionally offer your frog thawed rodents that are suitable for its size. Do not feed it only rodents, though, because that diet would be too heavy. It's better to provide a varied diet that includes insects.

- Dangle prey in front of the frog's mouth with tweezers, and the frog will gobble it up.

- At every other meal, before distributing the insects, sprinkle them with calcium for reptiles. This is important for the frog's growth.

HERCULES BEETLE

Dynastes hercules

NOTE: USDA PERMIT REQUIRED

(CENTRAL AMERICA, SOUTH AMERICA, AND THE CARIBBEAN

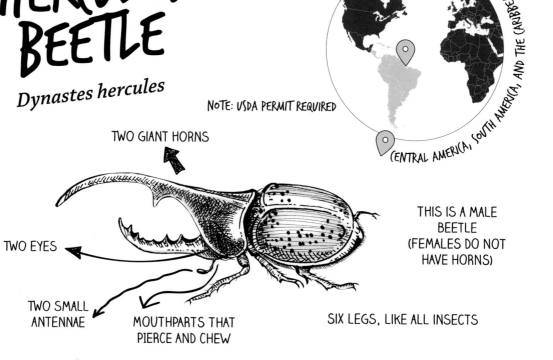

TWO GIANT HORNS

TWO EYES

TWO SMALL ANTENNAE

MOUTHPARTS THAT PIERCE AND CHEW

THIS IS A MALE BEETLE (FEMALES DO NOT HAVE HORNS)

SIX LEGS, LIKE ALL INSECTS

SIZE: UP TO 6 INCHES (15 CM) LONG

ORIGIN

This is the largest rhinoceros beetle in the world. It is an impressive and magnificent creature that lives in the wild in tropical forests. The Hercules beetle is nocturnal and spends its nights looking for ripe fruit to eat.

In Japan, coleopters (beetles) are very popular, and there are many stores where you can find everything you need for keeping pet beetles. But no matter where you live, you can find what you need for your beetle online, including protein to add to the soil in the tank to get really big larvae. People who breed beetles often want to raise their beetles to be as big as possible!

Have fun researching everything you can about these fascinating beetles so that you have the best chance of raising yours successfully. Because these beetles are so popular, it is unfortunately easy to find ones that have not been raised properly, so be sure to buy yours from a source that takes good care of their beetles.

- Like all beetles, Hercules beetles start off as larvae that live in dead and rotting tree trunks. These larvae, or grubs, are highly nutritious and a source of food for native people.

- This beetle is truly impressive for its size, weight, and unique appearance. It is pretty easy to raise in captivity as long as you have patience. You will have to be patient as you wait for your beetle to become an imago (a fully formed adult)—it takes up to two years for your larvae to grow into the largest beetle in the world. Yes—it's worth the wait!

- To speed up the process, you can buy grubs that are already several months old, but they will cost more. This species is not trendy, so you won't find it at the local pet-supply store. You can order grubs online from sources specializing in coleopters.

MY OBSERVATIONS

Start with a group of larvae. If you start with just one, and it dies after a few months, you will be discouraged. With a group, you increase your chances of ending up with imagos of both sexes.

HOUSING

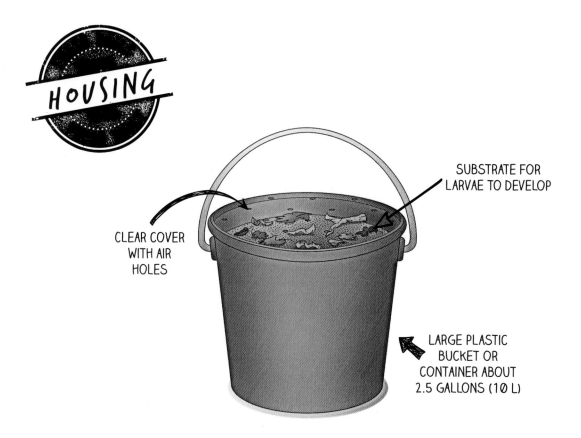

SUBSTRATE FOR LARVAE TO DEVELOP

CLEAR COVER WITH AIR HOLES

LARGE PLASTIC BUCKET OR CONTAINER ABOUT 2.5 GALLONS (10 L)

◆ Raising larvae is easy and low maintenance. For a few small larvae, you can start with a 2.5-gallon (10-L) plastic container. Pierce holes in the lid to provide adequate airflow.

◆ The quality of the substrate is very important for the larvae to grow properly. Here's the recipe: 70 percent ground decomposing wood, 20 percent ground oak leaves, and 10 percent organic soil without fertilizer. Mix it all together and then moisten it. The substrate should not be soaking wet. When you squeeze it, there shouldn't be any water dripping out.

◆ Add whole pieces of rotting oak to your mixture, and that's it. Your larvae will have enough to feed on for a few months. Once they have grown (because they will become huge, weighing up to 3.5 ounces [100 g] each!), you will need to separate them and provide each one with its own 2.5-gallon (10-L) container.

◆ One day, your larvae will start turning yellow. This means they are getting ready to become pupae. Each grub will form a cocoon and transform into a pupa inside. When the pupae come out of the cocoons, be prepared to find aliens in your home! Their bodies are very interesting looking. You will place each pupa in an artificial pupal chamber (available online), away from the light, with a fine layer of slightly moistened substrate. In a few months, they will transform into imagos. You can order these pupal chambers on the Internet.

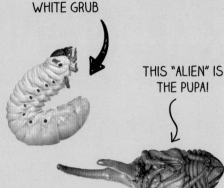

WHITE GRUB

THIS "ALIEN" IS THE PUPA!

CARE TIPS

There isn't much going on while the larvae grow! Each month, you can check to make sure all is well by looking through their substrate, but avoid disturbing them too much. Same thing for the pupae. Once they are settled in their chambers for metamorphosis (transformation into adult form), do not touch them, or else they may not develop properly into imagos.

➧ Finally, after all this time of patiently waiting, the big day arrives: you will see a magnificent giant beetle emerge. If it is a male, it will live only a few months, just long enough to reproduce with the female. (Note: Along with other differences in appearance, females do not have horns on their heads.)

➧ A female will lay eggs in an egg-laying chamber, which you must prepare. From these eggs, tiny larvae will hatch, and the cycle will begin again.

BLACK GARDEN ANT

Lasius niger

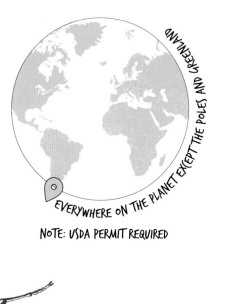

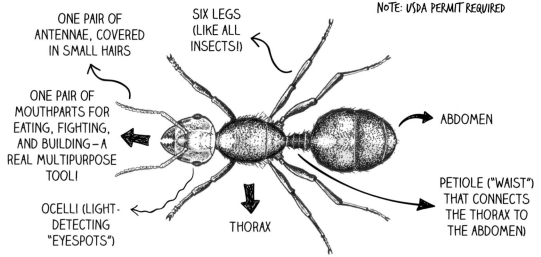

ONE PAIR OF ANTENNAE, COVERED IN SMALL HAIRS

SIX LEGS (LIKE ALL INSECTS!)

ONE PAIR OF MOUTHPARTS FOR EATING, FIGHTING, AND BUILDING – A REAL MULTIPURPOSE TOOL!

ABDOMEN

OCELLI (LIGHT-DETECTING "EYESPOTS")

THORAX

PETIOLE ("WAIST") THAT CONNECTS THE THORAX TO THE ABDOMEN)

ORIGIN

More than 12,000 species of ant have been recorded. Ants are native to almost everywhere in the world. Greenland and Antarctica are among the few places they are not found. They don't like the cold! The largest populations are concentrated in tropical regions and South America.

Ants are known for their highly developed and effective mode of communication using chemical substances called *pheromones* that their bodies produce. They emit different chemicals in different situations.

- Ants are so fun to keep and watch! These fascinating insects deserve a book of their own on how to raise them. They have complex societies and are often organized into castes, or social classes, each with a different role to play and job to do.

- The colony depends on the queen, which is the only egg-layer as well as the founder of the colony. If she stops laying eggs, the colony stops growing.

- Some species feed on other insects, some eat seeds, and others eat fungi (a type of mushroom) that they grow themselves—no, I'm not making this up! Other species protect and raise colonies of aphids, feeding on a substance called "honeydew" made by the aphids.

- Ants are incredible insects! You can spend hours observing a colony in an ant farm the size of a DVD case.

- Raising ants has become more and more popular, and it's become easier to find all of the supplies you need to properly raise and care for ants.

MY OBSERVATIONS
Ants don't like light in their tunnels! Place a piece of cardboard or thick cloth over the ant farm so they can live in the dark.

HOUSING

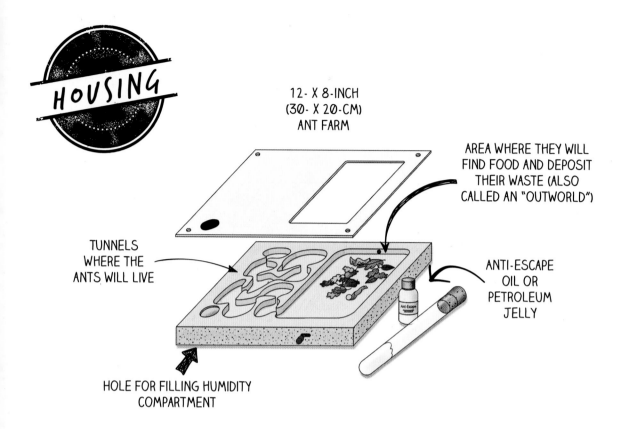

12- X 8-INCH
(30- X 20-CM)
ANT FARM

AREA WHERE THEY WILL FIND FOOD AND DEPOSIT THEIR WASTE (ALSO CALLED AN "OUTWORLD")

TUNNELS WHERE THE ANTS WILL LIVE

ANTI-ESCAPE OIL OR PETROLEUM JELLY

HOLE FOR FILLING HUMIDITY COMPARTMENT

◆ The container you use to raise your ants is called a farm. Ant farms can be found in all sizes, shapes, and styles and can be made out of a multitude of materials. The makers of ant farms are often very creative. You are sure to find one that you like and that your ants will like as well.

◆ Common species are not very expensive, but rare species can be too expensive for the beginner.

◆ You often start with a simple test tube containing a queen and a few workers. You will transfer this little group of ants to the farm once the colony starts to grow inside the tube.

◆ Species that are easier for beginners are often *Lasius niger* and *Messor barbarus*. They are not very demanding, they will tolerate beginners' mistakes, and they are quite hardy!

◆ Ants are a very good choice if you're just starting out and want to observe insects. They don't require a lot of care, and the cost of raising them, once you've bought the ant farm and the initial ants, is really minimal. Even children of nine or ten years old can successfully grow and keep ant colonies.

◆ Do-it-yourselfers can build their own ant farms by following online tutorials, which are easy to find. With the low cost of ant farms, however, it's better to start out by buying one, unless you want to risk finding the colony wandering around your living room!

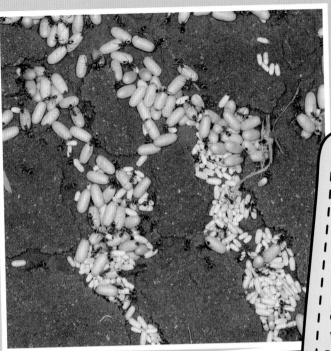

ANT LARVAE

CARE TIPS

The amount of heat and humidity your ants need depend on their species, so be sure to do your homework beforehand.

Don't forget to regularly apply the anti-escape product to the tops of the walls of the outworld (hunting area). If you do forget, escape is guaranteed!

GOLDEN SILK ORB-WEAVER

Nephila sp.

ALL TROPICAL REGIONS AROUND THE WORLD

EIGHT LEGS (LIKE ALL SPIDERS!)

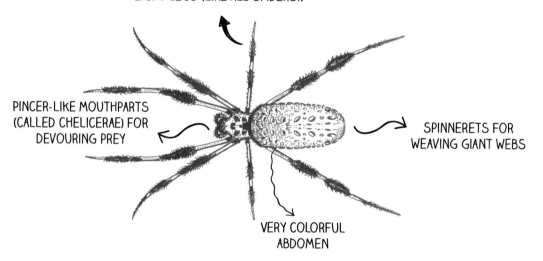

PINCER-LIKE MOUTHPARTS (CALLED CHELICERAE) FOR DEVOURING PREY

SPINNERETS FOR WEAVING GIANT WEBS

VERY COLORFUL ABDOMEN

ORIGIN

Golden silk orb-weavers can be found in tropical regions around the world. They weave giant webs—the largest in the world! These webs are dangerous traps for any insects that venture in. An orb-weaver can spin a huge web between two trees that measures several feet (more than a meter) across, leaving little chance for any creature wandering down its path.

- The female orb-weaver is impressive in size. It can measure up to several inches in length (7 to 8 cm), legs not included.

- The male is much smaller and often shares the female's web, living on the opposite side and eating her leftovers.

- This species, although it produces venom like all spiders, is not dangerous to humans.

- It won't be easy for your family members to accept this type of pet if they are afraid of spiders, but if you do manage to convince them, it is a magnificent species that is really interesting to watch.

- Be careful! This spider is fragile, so avoid handling it.

MY OBSERVATIONS
Good luck persuading your family to allow a giant spider to live free in your living room!

HOUSING

IN A CORNER OF THE LIVING ROOM OR YOUR BEDROOM, IN FREEDOM!

PLANT FOR ANCHORING THE WEB

So far, so good! You have finally convinced your family that keeping spiders is super-cool, but here's where things might get complicated...

◆ From experience, I know that these spiders don't like being in terrariums, because they need room to weave. So, the best place to raise them is in the open, in your bedroom or your living room. You'll have to be very persuasive!

◆ If that fails, you can use a "flexarium," a sort of terrarium with mesh netting instead of walls. Get a large one that measures at least 24 x 24 x 48 inches (60 x 60 x 120 cm). The best setup, however, is to allow the spider to weave its web freely in a room.

◆ Once the spider weaves its web, it won't leave the web, so you don't have to worry about finding it walking around your house.

◆ When you buy the spider, set it free near a plant. It will anchor its web between the plant, a wall, and the ceiling, and you'll have a little corner of jungle in your home!

◆ The golden silk orb-weaver requires a temperature of between 68 and 81° Fahrenheit (20 and 27° Celsius), depending on the species, so be sure to research the type of spider you have chosen.

FEEDING

- This spider is easy to feed. Toss one or two insects into its web every week. It likes crickets, but even grasshoppers in summer or mealworms will do.

- For drinking water, spray one part of its web once or twice a week.

MOMBO ASSASSIN BUG

Platymeris sp. "Mombo"

TANZANIA

NOTE: REQUIRES USDA PERMIT AND
APPROVED CONTAINMENT

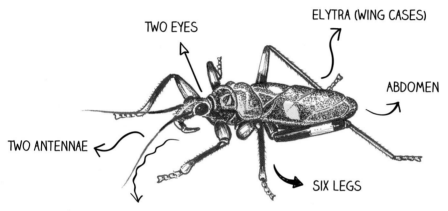

TWO EYES

ELYTRA (WING CASES)

ABDOMEN

TWO ANTENNAE

SIX LEGS

ROSTRUM (POWERFUL ORGAN
THAT PIERCES PREY AND INJECTS
IT WITH VENOMOUS SALIVA)

SIZE: UP TO 1½ INCHES (3.5 CM)

ORIGIN

Their name suits them so well! These insects that are
native to Africa are killers. They are nocturnal and
always hungry.

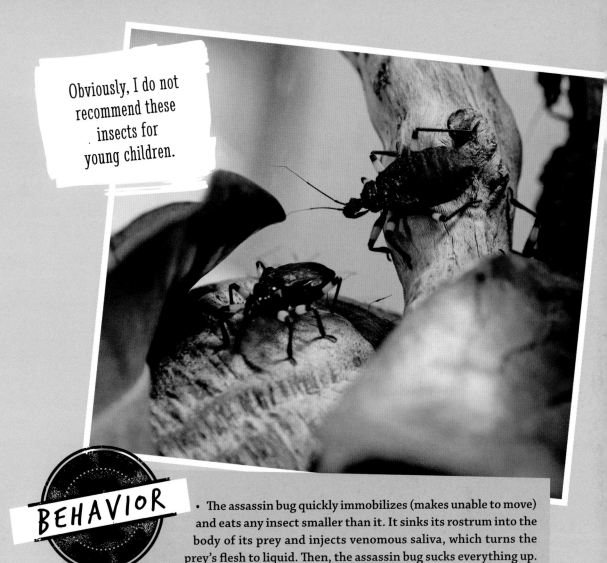

Obviously, I do not recommend these insects for young children.

BEHAVIOR

- The assassin bug quickly immobilizes (makes unable to move) and eats any insect smaller than it. It sinks its rostrum into the body of its prey and injects venomous saliva, which turns the prey's flesh to liquid. Then, the assassin bug sucks everything up. Not so nice!

- Assassin bugs are shy during the day and will often remain hidden. But, once night falls, they go hunting for crickets, mealworms, small cockroaches, and the like.

- These miniature predators are very interesting to observe and super-easy to raise. This species lives about one and a half years.

HOUSING

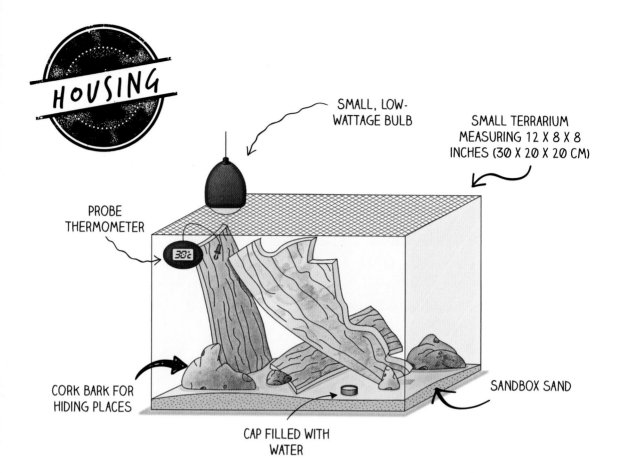

SMALL, LOW-WATTAGE BULB

SMALL TERRARIUM MEASURING 12 X 8 X 8 INCHES (30 X 20 X 20 CM)

PROBE THERMOMETER

30°

CORK BARK FOR HIDING PLACES

CAP FILLED WITH WATER

SANDBOX SAND

◆ Assassin bugs are easy to raise in a small terrarium, where you create a hot, dry environment for them.

◆ Using a small heating mat for reptiles or a small, low-wattage bulb, heat the terrarium to 84 to 86° Fahrenheit (29 to 30° Celsius) during the day. At night, turn it off to allow the temperature to drop to 68 to 72° Fahrenheit (20 to 22° Celsius).

◆ A base of coarse sand, a few rocks for decoration and climbing, one or two pieces of bark for hiding places—and that's it! You've made a habitat that will suit them very nicely.

◆ Assassin bugs live in groups, so start with at least four or five. If they mate, you will find eggs, which you can incubate in a small plastic box with air holes in the lid and slightly damp substrate. Leave the box inside the terrarium to benefit from the warmth inside.

◆ You can raise the young either in a separate tank, set up the same way as the parents' tank, or in the main tank. If you keep them in the tank with the parents, feed the adults plenty so they will not eat the youngsters.

FEEDING

- Small crickets or vinegar flies will be perfect for feeding the young assassin bugs at the start.

- Crickets, mealworms, and small cockroaches are the adults' favorite prey.

CARE TIPS

Offer water in a small plastic bottle cap, even though they get most of their hydration from their prey. Once a week, spray a little water in one of the corners of the terrarium.

MY OBSERVATIONS

These impressive predators are a fun species to raise and watch, and their tank setup doesn't cost a lot.

GUINEA PIG

Cavia porcellus

ANDES MOUNTAIN RANGE

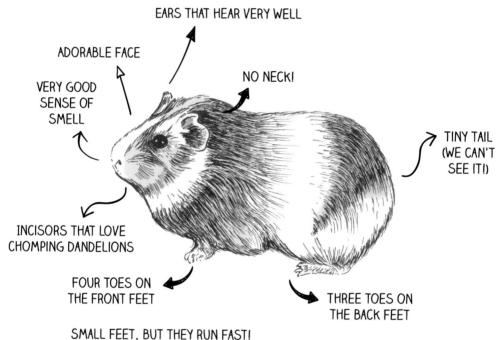

EARS THAT HEAR VERY WELL

ADORABLE FACE

NO NECK!

VERY GOOD SENSE OF SMELL

TINY TAIL (WE CAN'T SEE IT!)

INCISORS THAT LOVE CHOMPING DANDELIONS

FOUR TOES ON THE FRONT FEET

THREE TOES ON THE BACK FEET

SMALL FEET, BUT THEY RUN FAST!

ORIGIN

So cute! That's usually what people say when they see a guinea pig! The species name does not indicate their origin, the Andes mountain range in South America, where they are very popular—for their meat. Guinea pigs in the Andes have been raised for food for a very long time.

BEHAVIOR

- The guinea pig is diurnal (awake during the day). It lives in small groups and does not like to live alone. It is a calm rodent and does not trust strangers.

- This popular pet needs space and a special diet.

- Because guinea pigs do not like living alone, you need to adopt two, and three would be even better. Choose a group of females so you will not end up having to raise guinea pig babies that you're not ready for.

- Guinea pigs are often afraid when they first go to their new homes. You need to help yours trust you slowly and gently. Offer them little bits of fruit or vegetables by hand to make them want to approach you. Do not make quick or rough movements.

- Let them get out to stretch their legs every day by opening the door of their cage. Choose a cage with an opening on the side so they can leave and then return on their own.

- Guinea pigs can jump, but they can't climb.

- They vocalize a lot to communicate with each other and to express how they feel, for example, when they are content. You'll notice, when you approach their cage with food, that they let you know they're looking forward to a feast!

MY OBSERVATIONS
Today you can find an amazing variety of guinea pigs, including long-haired Angoras, Abyssinians with hair that grows in circular "rosettes," and "Skinnies" that look like little hippopotamuses because they have no hair at all! All of the different types get along with each other.

HOUSING

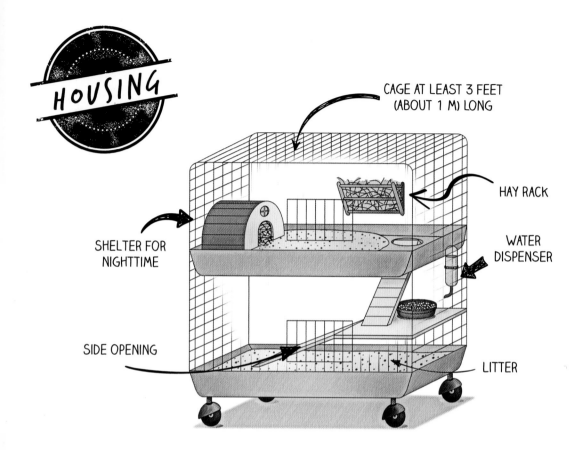

CAGE AT LEAST 3 FEET (ABOUT 1 M) LONG

HAY RACK

WATER DISPENSER

SHELTER FOR NIGHTTIME

SIDE OPENING

LITTER

◆ Get a cage at least 3 feet (about 1 m) long so that multiple guinea pigs will be comfortable and have enough space.

◆ Place the cage away from drafts, either on the floor or on a piece of low furniture. Because they are active during the day and sleep at night, they won't keep you awake at night if you put the cage in your bedroom.

◆ Use hemp, flax, or coconut fiber litter. Keep the litter clean by changing it regularly.

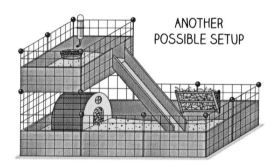

ANOTHER POSSIBLE SETUP

◆ In summer, your guinea pigs can spend some time in a safe enclosure outdoors, because they love eating grass and playing. Make sure that the enclosure has a shady area and fresh water at all times.

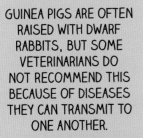

GUINEA PIG

GUINEA PIGS ARE OFTEN RAISED WITH DWARF RABBITS, BUT SOME VETERINARIANS DO NOT RECOMMEND THIS BECAUSE OF DISEASES THEY CAN TRANSMIT TO ONE ANOTHER.

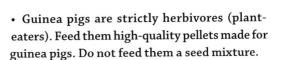

FEEDING

- Guinea pigs are strictly herbivores (plant-eaters). Feed them high-quality pellets made for guinea pigs. Do not feed them a seed mixture.

- Offer them vegetables you have washed and dried, wild grasses (they love dandelion!), and clover. You can add some fruit to their diet as well. The more you vary their food, the healthier they will be.

- Because guinea pigs have trouble absorbing vitamin C, you need to add extra vitamin C to their diets to make sure they are getting enough. Give them oranges cut in quarters, for example, or liquid vitamin C, which you can buy at a pet-supply store.

- Keep good-quality hay in their cage at all times. Place it in a small hayrack so that it stays clean. Guinea pigs not only eat this hay, but they use it to keep their teeth from growing too much. The hay works like a file to wear their teeth down.

GIANT AFRICAN LAND SNAIL

Achatina fulica

TROPICAL AFRICA, CARIBBEAN

NOTE: ILLEGAL TO KEEP THROUGHOUT UNITED STATES AND REGULATED IN CANADA

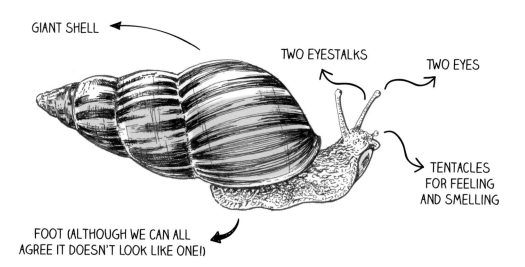

GIANT SHELL ←

TWO EYESTALKS

TWO EYES

TENTACLES FOR FEELING AND SMELLING

FOOT (ALTHOUGH WE CAN ALL AGREE IT DOESN'T LOOK LIKE ONE!)

ORIGIN

This snail is native to the tropical regions of Africa and has also found its way to the Caribbean islands, where it thrives. It likes a hot and humid environment and is a source of food in many countries.

It is an omnivore and an opportunist, meaning that it will eat just about anything it finds, whether plant or animal. Of course, the animals it eats are often dead. We're talking about a snail, after all, that couldn't catch a mouse on the run!

In the snail family, this one is truly gigantic. This is an impressive species whose shell can measure almost 8 inches (20 cm) long!

BEHAVIOR

- This spectacular snail is definitely not a demanding pet. It is easy to take care of and is perfect for beginners.

WARNING!

Know where your snail comes from! Snails raised in captivity do not have parasites, but some imported wild species can carry parasites and germs that are harmful to humans. Even though cases of infection are very rare, wash your hands thoroughly and use alcohol-based hand sanitizer after each time you handle your snail.

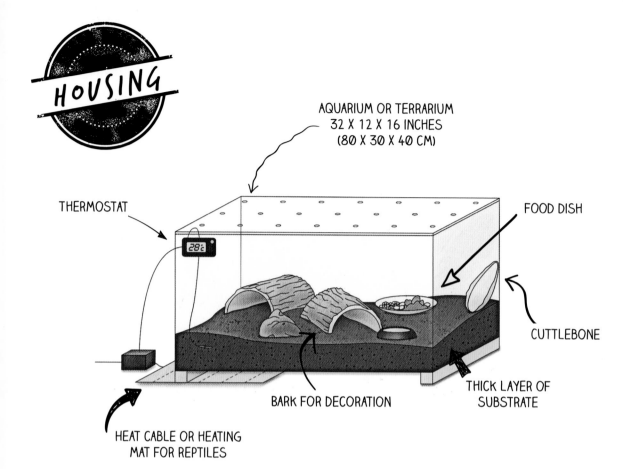

HOUSING

AQUARIUM OR TERRARIUM
32 X 12 X 16 INCHES
(80 X 30 X 40 CM)

THERMOSTAT

28℃

FOOD DISH

CUTTLEBONE

BARK FOR DECORATION

THICK LAYER OF SUBSTRATE

HEAT CABLE OR HEATING MAT FOR REPTILES

◆ It's very easy to keep this snail as long as you have a large enough tank. A terrarium or aquarium, or even a large plastic bin with air holes in the cover, will do the job. If you have a tank with an open top, keep it partially covered with a piece of plexiglass so that the environment does not dry out too quickly.

◆ At the bottom, lay a thick layer of coconut fiber humus, several inches (7 to 8 cm) deep. Spray it regularly to keep it damp.

◆ Keep the temperature at 82° Fahrenheit (28° Celsius) by using a heating mat or cable, connected to a thermostat, under the tank. At night, program your thermostat for 73° Fahrenheit (23° Celsius), a slightly lower temperature that the snail will like.

◆ Snails are hermaphrodites, meaning that they are male and female at the same time. If you have two snails, you will soon find eggs. Incubate the eggs in a smaller container filled with damp coconut fiber. Place this container in the parents' tank so that the eggs benefit from the higher temperature. A few weeks later, miniature replicas of the parents will hatch.

CARE TIPS

Spraying lukewarm water in the tank in the morning and at night will give you a chance to watch the snail's activity.

FEEDING

- The giant African land snail will eat anything!

- Wash fruits and vegetables thoroughly to remove any pesticides. Offer pieces of fruits and vegetables in a dish along with high-quality dry dog or cat food that does not contain vitamin D3 (cholecalciferol).

- Replace the food every day to prevent mold from developing in this tropical environment.

- Always make sure there is a cuttlebone available to provide calcium. It's very important for your snail to get calcium regularly so it can grow.

RED CHERRY SHRIMP

Neocaridina heteropoda

TAIWAN

NOTE: RESTRICTED IN MAINE; PERMIT REQUIRED

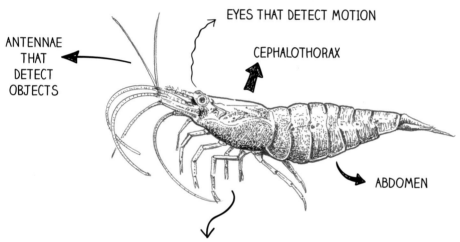

EYES THAT DETECT MOTION

ANTENNAE THAT DETECT OBJECTS

CEPHALOTHORAX

ABDOMEN

SMALL LEGS FOR SWIMMING
(CALLED PLEOPODS)

ORIGIN

The shrimp that live in the rivers of Taiwan are more or less transparent (clear). Over the years, breeders have worked to produce more colorful shrimp in shades of red, yellow, black, and blue. They are all the same species—its's just the different colors that make them look different.

- These shrimp are becoming stars of the aquarium world. They've become very popular, and it's easy to see why: they come in cool colors, they are easy to raise, and they are easy to breed.

- The red cherry shrimp is very social and lives in groups.

- This shrimp is mainly an algivore (algae eater) but is also a detrivore (eater of dead organic/plant matter). Basically, it eats water weeds and anything else it finds in the aquarium. It is constantly in search of food.

- If you add fish—even tiny ones—to the aquarium, they will definitely eat the baby shrimp. I recommend keeping only shrimp in the tank, although a few aquatic snails can live with your shrimp with no problem.

- These shrimp are always in motion, wandering between the bottom of the tank and the water's surface, which makes the aquarium very pretty and interesting to watch.

MY OBSERVATIONS

Choose a color of shrimp that you like and stick with that color. If you mix colors, the offspring will come out transparent. If you keep only red shrimp in the tank, however, their offspring will be red as well.

HOUSING

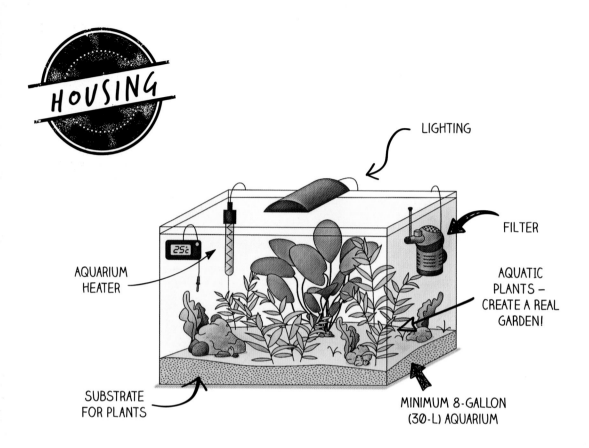

LIGHTING

FILTER

AQUATIC PLANTS – CREATE A REAL GARDEN!

AQUARIUM HEATER

SUBSTRATE FOR PLANTS

MINIMUM 8-GALLON (30-L) AQUARIUM

◆ These shrimp *need* aquatic plants. They will feed on the microscopic algae that live on the plants and will explore the plants all day long. Thus, you need to first grow a real aquatic garden in the tank before you add the shrimp.

◆ Spread a layer of substrate made for aquatic plants at the bottom of the tank. Cover this layer with about an inch (a few centimeters) of fine aquarium sand (rinse it well under running water first).

◆ Place a small filter about an inch (a few centimeters) below the top of the tank and add a small heater (1 watt per liter of water) that you will set to 75° Fahrenheit (24° Celsius) once the tank is filled with water. Install lighting that is suitable for aquatic plants.

◆ It's time to start your garden, so get a lot of plants! Red cherry shrimp like plants with thin leaves, like hygrophila (swampweed), cryptocoryne, and pogostemon, as well as moss, such as Java moss, that you can attach to aquarium stones with fishing net. It will grow on top and look very pretty!

◆ It's easier to plant before you fill your aquarium with water, but it's important to regularly spray water during the planting process to prevent the environment from drying out. Note: If using tap water to fill your aquarium, the water must first sit in a bucket for twenty-four hours to remove the chlorine.

◆ Remove the stone wool in which the plants are wrapped as well as the weights meant to hold them to the bottom of the tank. Rinse the plants well and insert each stem deep into the substrate with tweezers.

◆ Be creative in your planting—just remember to arrange the small plants in the front of the tank and the large plants in the back.

◆ When you are finished planting, fill the aquarium with water. Place a small dish at the bottom of the tank and slowly pour the water into the dish so that you don't destroy your plants.

◆ Once the tank is filled, plug in the filter and heater and let them run for at least three weeks. This gives the plants time to grow and the water to become balanced. Be patient during this time. (Patience is very important for an aquarium lover!)

◆ Connect the lamp to a small timer. Start with seven hours of light per day—any longer than that, and algae might take over. Later, gradually increase the lighting to up to ten hours per day.

◆ Place your aquarium in a dark corner of a room, never in direct sunlight.

◆ Three weeks later, introduce your group of shrimp—at least six to ten individuals—to their new home. First, soak the bag containing the shrimp in the aquarium for twenty minutes so the water temperatures can balance. Then, every five minutes, slowly pour a tiny amount of water from the tank into the bag so your shrimp can get used to the tank water. After thirty minutes, use a small fish net to release the shrimp into the aquarium.

◆ After a few weeks, you should see female shrimp carrying eggs under their abdomens. They are said to be "berried." Miniature shrimp will hatch from these eggs.

CARE TIPS

Change the water regularly—about 10 percent of the volume of the aquarium at a time—every two weeks.

Shrimp molt (shed their skin) regularly as they grow. If you find the shed skin, don't panic. If it's transparent, it's not a dead shrimp!

FEEDING

- After two or three days, when the shrimp are used to their new home, you can start feeding them: a carrot shaving, the end of a cucumber, one or two shrimp pellets—small quantities for their small stomachs. If you overfeed them, the tank water will become dirty.

- At the beginning, feed them four times a week. You can feed them more often as your population grows.

ORANGE DWARF ((PO) CRAYFISH

Cambarellus patzcuarensis var. "Orange"

MEXICO
(LAKE
PÁTZCUARO)

NOTE: RESTRICTED IN MAINE;
PERMIT REQUIRED

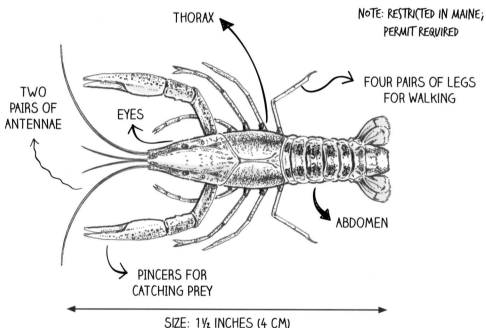

THORAX

FOUR PAIRS OF LEGS
FOR WALKING

TWO
PAIRS OF
ANTENNAE

EYES

ABDOMEN

PINCERS FOR
CATCHING PREY

SIZE: 1½ INCHES (4 CM)

ORIGIN

This dwarf crayfish is endemic to Lake Pátzcuaro, in the Mexican state of Michoacán. This means that, in the wild, this is the only location they live in.

In the wild, they are not orange, like the ones you find in pet-supply stores, but rather brownish. Breeders have made it possible to produce crayfish with this flashy orange color.

BEHAVIOR

- These Mexican crayfish must always be kept in aquariums. It is important that these exotic beauties never end up in our rivers!

- They can live in a group and are not aggressive toward one another.

- They are very opportunistic when it comes to food, which means that they will eat just about anything they find. They are also rather adaptable when it comes to temperature and water quality, which makes them easy to raise.

- You may read that these crayfish can live with other fish, but remember that they are opportunistic (which helps them survive in the wild). If one of them can catch a fish with its pincers, it will. So I recommend that you raise your crayfish in a little group of crayfish only.

MY OBSERVATIONS
Add a few aquatic snails to the tank to clean up the algae that grows on the glass.

HOUSING

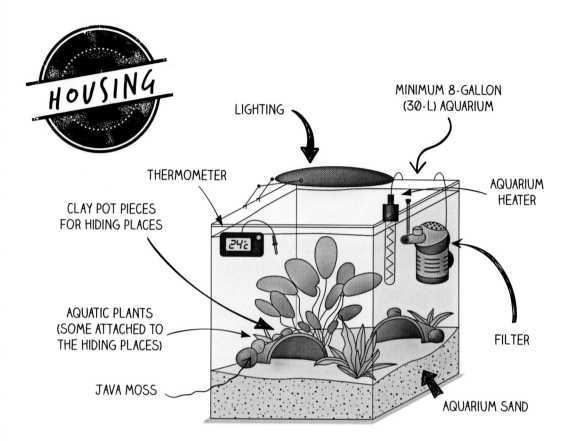

LIGHTING

MINIMUM 8-GALLON (30-L) AQUARIUM

THERMOMETER

AQUARIUM HEATER

CLAY POT PIECES FOR HIDING PLACES

24°C

AQUATIC PLANTS (SOME ATTACHED TO THE HIDING PLACES)

FILTER

JAVA MOSS

AQUARIUM SAND

◆ An 8-gallon (30-L) aquarium will work for a group of four individuals. The surface area of the tank is more important than the height. An aquarium for turtles, one that is longer and wider than it is tall, will do the job.

◆ As with any aquarium, you will have to prepare the tank and wait before introducing your crayfish. Refer to the pages on the red cherry shrimp or the Siamese fighting fish to understand why it's important to wait a few weeks once your aquarium is set up.

◆ Set up your aquarium in the following way:
1. Put a layer of natural aquarium sand, rinsed thoroughly, in the bottom of the tank.

2. Position some clay pot pieces to make hiding places, which your crayfish will like. Set up as many hiding places as you have crayfish, or even more.

3. Use fishing line or super-glue gel (watch out for your fingers!) to attach epiphyte plants, such as anubias, to these pots. These types of plants grow on objects and do not need substrate, so they will make the hiding places look very nice. This also works very well with Java moss.

4. Set the heater to 75° Fahrenheit (24° Celsius).

5. Place the filter so that it sits about an inch (a few centimeters) below the surface of the water.

6. Fill the aquarium with tap water that has sat for twenty-four hours beforehand.

ORANGE DWARF ((PO) CRAYFISH

➧ Use a mechanical timer for the lighting. Start with seven hours of light a day and increase it gradually over a few weeks until you get up to ten hours a day.

➧ Your crayfish will molt (shed their skin) regularly, and they are unprotected during molting. They will hide to avoid the others, which is why it is important to have plenty of hiding places and plants.

CARE TIPS

Your crayfish will start having babies quickly, so feed the parents well to keep them from eating their offspring. The young will start by feeding on microscopic waste and organisms that have grown in the aquarium. Be careful, because the young crayfish may also turn cannibalistic (start to eat each other) if they don't get enough to eat.

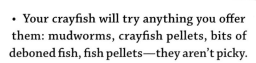

FEEDING

• Your crayfish will try anything you offer them: mudworms, crayfish pellets, bits of deboned fish, fish pellets—they aren't picky.

• Feed them six days per week. One day each week, let them fast (go without food).

CHINESE FIRE-BELLIED NEWT

Cynops or *Hypselotriton orientalis*

CHINA

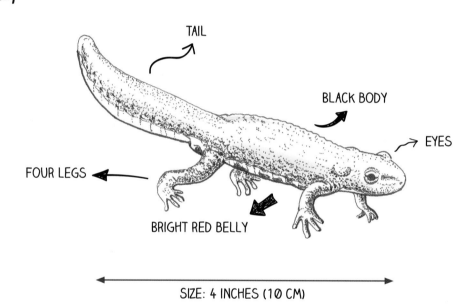

TAIL

BLACK BODY

EYES

FOUR LEGS

BRIGHT RED BELLY

SIZE: 4 INCHES (10 CM)

ORIGIN

This pretty little newt lives in small groups in calm waters in China. It starts its life on land, in a humid environment. Once it is an adult, it becomes almost 100 percent aquatic.

BEHAVIOR

- This species does not breathe underwater but returns regularly to the water's surface to breathe air.

- These newts are easy to raise, but they don't like heat or a strong water current.

- For your newts to live long lives, you must let them hibernate at a temperature of 46 to 50° Fahrenheit (8 to 10° Celsius). If you have a garage or basement, place the tank in this cool place for two months during the winter. Reduce the lighting for several hours per day and stop feeding them during hibernation. They will appreciate it.

  - Slowly lower the temperature as you prepare for hibernation, and then slowly increase the amount of lighting and raise the temperature as you prepare to take them out of hibernation.

MY OBSERVATIONS
If you take good care of them, your newts can live for more than twenty years!

HOUSING

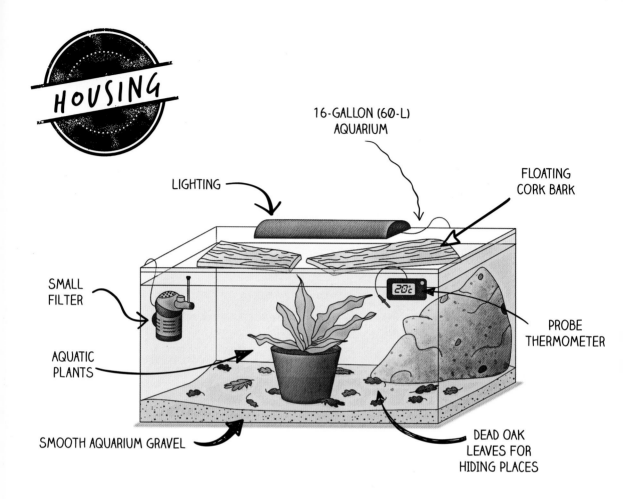

16-GALLON (60-L) AQUARIUM

LIGHTING

FLOATING CORK BARK

SMALL FILTER

20°C

PROBE THERMOMETER

AQUATIC PLANTS

SMOOTH AQUARIUM GRAVEL

DEAD OAK LEAVES FOR HIDING PLACES

◆ A 16-gallon (60-L) aquarium, three-quarters filled with water, is good for a group of four newts.

◆ Spread a layer of gravel that you have thoroughly rinsed first. Add hiding places, including dead oak leaves, in the bottom of the tank. These leaves also help to make the water's pH slightly acidic, which the newts will like.

◆ Add plenty of aquatic plants. A good choice is the elodea. It's hardy, it's pretty, and it likes a fairly cool environment.

◆ Lighting will help the plants grow. Newts don't like bright light, so start with a few extra elodea plants floating on the surface to filter the light.

◆ Place a small filter in the tank. Make sure it's not too powerful, because newts don't like strong water currents. You do not need a heater, because the newts live at room temperature.

◆ Add a few pieces of cork bark to float on the surface so the newts can climb out of the water if they want to, even though it probably won't be often.

CHINESE FIRE-BELLIED NEWT

DAPHNIA, SEEN UNDER
A MICROSCOPE

CARE TIPS
Gammarus (scuds) and daphnia
are little creatures that will help
maintain your cold-water aquarium—
they make a super cleaning team, and
your newts will enjoy snacking on
them now and then!

FEEDING

• Small earthworms are a very good food for
this species. You can switch them up from time
to time with mudworms, which you will find
frozen or live at your local pet-supply store.

AXOLOTL

Ambystoma mexicanum

NOTE: ILLEGAL TO KEEP IN (ALIFORNIA, MAINE, NEW JERSEY, AND VIRGINIA; LEGAL TO KEEP IN NEW MEXICO BUT ILLEGAL TO IMPORT

MEXICO (XOCHIMILCO)

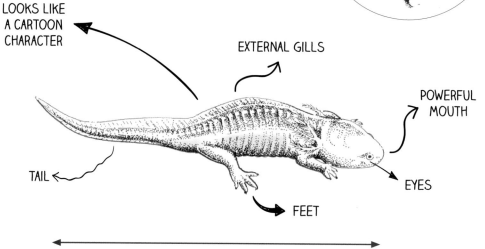

LOOKS LIKE A CARTOON CHARACTER

EXTERNAL GILLS

POWERFUL MOUTH

TAIL

FEET

EYES

SIZE: 8 TO 10 INCHES (20 TO 25 CM)

ORIGIN

The axolotl is native to the Xochimilco wetlands of Mexico. It is the only place where this creature can be found in the wild.

Nicknamed the "Mexican walking fish," it is not a fish but a salamander. It spends its life in larva mode, without ever maturing into an adult salamander (except in very rare cases). In the larval stage, it can live for more than twenty years underwater.

This is an endangered species in the wild. All specimens on the pet market are raised by breeders and do not threaten the Mexican population of axolotls. The axolotl has become very popular as a pet. Who wouldn't like having a cartoon character living in his or her home?

BEHAVIOR

- In addition to staying at the larval stage for its entire life, this salamander has superhero powers that fascinate scientists: it can regenerate. It has the ability to regrow almost any part of its body, including its limbs and even parts of its brain.

- These salamanders are really endearing and very interesting to observe. Many different colors of axolotls are available on the market, from albinos that are all white with red gills (the most popular) to golden or melanistic (appearing all black). There's one for every preference, and you can mix them without worry.

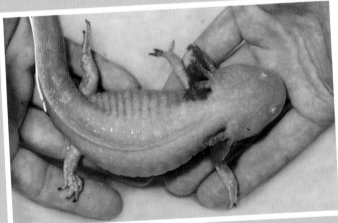

MY OBSERVATIONS

Young axolotls can be cannibalistic at times. Feed them as much as they want every day. If they do not get enough food, they will soon start to attack one another.

HOUSING

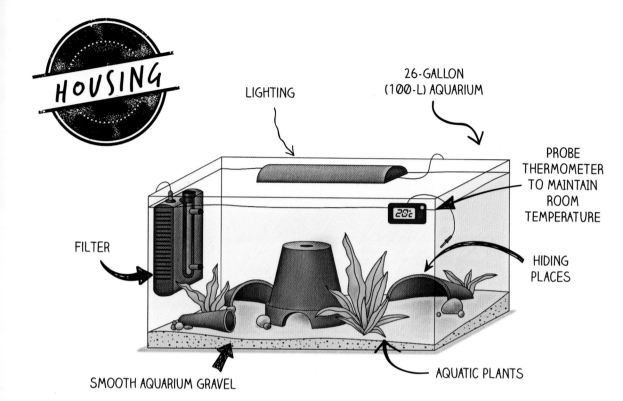

LIGHTING

26-GALLON
(100-L) AQUARIUM

PROBE
THERMOMETER
TO MAINTAIN
ROOM
TEMPERATURE

20℃

FILTER

HIDING
PLACES

AQUATIC PLANTS

SMOOTH AQUARIUM GRAVEL

◆ Axolotls have an enemy: heat. They don't like it, and it can kill them. You must keep them at room temperature. If your home gets hot in summer, you must find a way to keep them cool. The ideal temperature for them is 68° Fahrenheit (20° Celsius).

◆ You will need a 26-gallon (100-L) aquarium for a group of three axolotls, because they live in groups. They can grow to a length of 8 to 10 inches (20 to 25 cm), so they need space. A layer of about an inch (2 to 3 cm) of smooth aquarium gravel on the bottom of the aquarium will be perfect.

◆ Set up plenty of hiding places for them. If you use clay pot pieces, make sure they have no sharp edges that can cut your pets' fragile skin.

◆ Add bunches of aquatic plants to filter the light. Axolotls don't like bright light.

◆ A filter suitable for the size of the aquarium will help provide good-quality water, which is important. Fill the tank with tap water that you've let sit for twenty-four hours.

◆ Complete the setup with lighting that will encourage the plants to grow. Connect the lighting to a timer set to eight to ten hours of light per day.

◆ Well-developed gills are a sign of good health in axolotls. When it's hot, if the temperature in the tank rises too high, the salamanders will not feel well. The first sign is their gills, which will look less developed. When you see this sign, you must quickly cool the aquarium water. One way is by floating ice packs on the surface (replace them regularly).

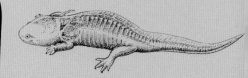

CARE TIPS

Replace 20 percent of the tank water every ten days. Before you discard the old water, use it to clean the filter. This way, you will save the good bacteria in your filter, which is necessary for the filter to work properly. If you wash the filter under running tap water, the chlorine in the water will kill all of the good bacteria, and that's not good for your tank.

FEEDING

• Axolotls feed on invertebrates (creatures without backbones), such as earthworms. When they are young, they love mudworms.

• You can also feed them pellets made for axolotls, which they usually like, along with bits of deboned fish.

LEOPARD GECKO

Eublepharis macularius

PAKISTAN, AFGHANISTAN, NORTHERN INDIA

NOTE: ILLEGAL TO KEEP IN HAWAII

CHUBBY TAIL

EYES

NOSTRILS

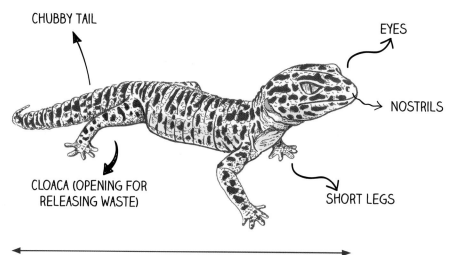

CLOACA (OPENING FOR RELEASING WASTE)

SHORT LEGS

SIZE: 8 INCHES (20 CM)

ORIGIN

The leopard gecko is a nocturnal animal that is native to the desert plains of Afghanistan, Pakistan, and India. In the wild, it lives in small harems (groups with one male and several females) and only goes out in the evenings to hunt. It's one of the most popular reptile pets and surely the most commonly bred reptile in the world, along with the bearded dragon (*Pogona vitticeps*).

- This gecko is easy to take care of and fairly small. A fat, well-developed tail is a sign of good health, while a thin tail is not normal for this species.

- Hundreds of colors and different patterns have been developed by breeders around the world. To me, however, the prettiest leopard gecko is one with its original coloring, even though it may be hard to find today.

- Reptiles usually don't like being handled, but leopard geckos can get used to it. Handle your gecko for short periods, twenty minutes at the most, and always over a table or couch because a fall could injure it.

MY OBSERVATIONS
Never catch your gecko by the tail—the tail could come off in your hand!

HOUSING

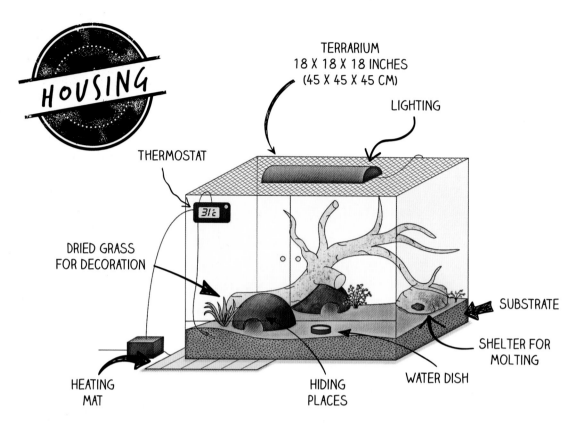

THERMOSTAT

TERRARIUM
18 X 18 X 18 INCHES
(45 X 45 X 45 CM)

LIGHTING

DRIED GRASS
FOR DECORATION

SUBSTRATE

SHELTER FOR
MOLTING

HEATING
MAT

HIDING
PLACES

WATER DISH

◆ A terrarium of 18 x 18 x 18 inches (45 x 45 x 45 cm) is good for one gecko. I recommend that you raise your gecko alone. If you have a couple, the male may bother the female by wanting to mate all the time. If you have two females, they will have dominance issues. So pick either a male or a female, but you can have only one!

◆ Be creative with the landscape! Different levels will make it more appealing.

◆ On the bottom of the tank, lay substrate that your gecko can't ingest—this is important! Sand alone could quickly cause a blockage in your gecko's body. Use a mixture of organic earth (70 percent) and sand (30 percent), and pack it down by pressing hard with your hands, or use a substrate made specifically for desert reptiles.

◆ Lightly spray the substrate when you are ready to place your gecko inside. Pack it down and let it dry, and it will become more solid, which will help prevent your gecko from eating it.

◆ Add bunches of dried grass for a natural look.

◆ Your gecko must be able to regulate its own temperature, so prepare two zones in the terrarium:
  1. Create a hot zone by placing a heating mat for reptiles under one-third of the terrarium. Connect the mat to a thermostat so you can control the temperature in this zone, keeping it at about 86 to 89° Fahrenheit (30 to 32° Celsius).
  2. The rest of the terrarium should be a cool zone of about 75 to 77° Fahrenheit (24 to 25° Celsius).

◆ Hiding places in both zones are very important so that your gecko can rest in either the hot or cooler area. Your gecko needs to sleep quietly during the day where no one can see it. There are many ways to make hiding places: cork bark, pieces of clay pots, special reptile shelters from the pet-supply store, and more.

◆ Provide lighting for eleven hours per day to recreate a day/night cycle.

◆ Set up a shallow water dish and change the water often. Reptiles like clean water as much as we do.

CARE TIPS

Your gecko may live up to twenty years! It will molt (shed its skin) throughout its life, more often when it is young. To help it molt properly, set up a molting shelter in the terrarium. One example is a plastic container with slightly damp substrate, such as coconut fiber and spaghnum moss, and a large enough opening for it to enter and exit easily. The humidity inside will help the skin shed.

FEEDING

• Your gecko is an insectivore, meaning that it eats insects. Live crickets, cockroaches, and small grasshoppers make a good diet.

• Feed your gecko in the evenings. Before you put the insects in the tank, sprinkle them with calcium powder enriched with vitamin D, available at pet-supply stores. This is important for your gecko's health.

BANDED (WHEELER'S) KNOB-TAILED GECKO

Nephrurus wheeleri cinctus

AUSTRALIA

NOTE: ILLEGAL TO KEEP IN HAWAII

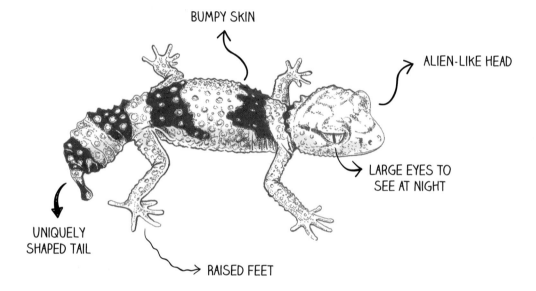

BUMPY SKIN

ALIEN-LIKE HEAD

LARGE EYES TO
SEE AT NIGHT

UNIQUELY
SHAPED TAIL

RAISED FEET

ORIGIN

Nephrurus wheeleri cinctus, the banded knob-tailed gecko (or Wheeler's knob-tailed gecko), is a small gecko that measures up to 5 inches (12 cm) long. It is native to the Australian outback.

These geckos are nocturnal. They aren't too popular with reptile keepers and are much less common than their cousin, the leopard gecko. It's too bad, because they are very attractive, calm, and easy to raise.

BEHAVIOR

- These geckos are fun to watch. When they see prey or meet another gecko, they communicate their excitement with their tail movements—a little like a dog wagging its tail!

- The genus *Nephrurus* includes many species: some with smooth skin, such as *Nephrurus levis*, which is harder to raise, and others with rough skin, such as *Nephrurus amyae*. *Nephrurus wheeleri* is the easiest gecko to raise in this attractive family.

- They don't like being handled, so avoid touching them as much as possible. They will thank you for leaving them in peace.

- This species can reproduce fairly easily after hibernating for a few months at about 59° Fahrenheit (15° Celsius).

MY OBSERVATIONS

You'll need a little luck to find one of these geckos—you will not see them at your local pet store. Look online for breeders, such as in reptile-keeper Facebook groups, and be patient.

HOUSING

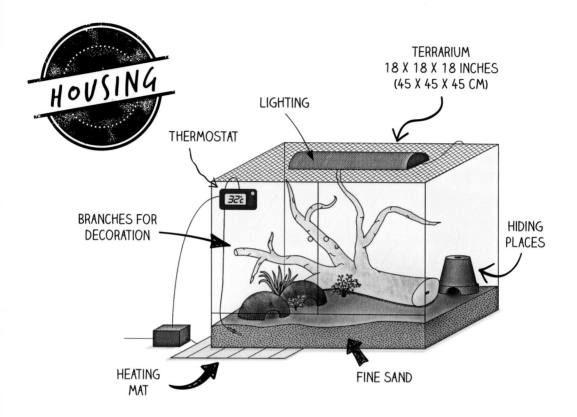

TERRARIUM
18 X 18 X 18 INCHES
(45 X 45 X 45 CM)

LIGHTING

THERMOSTAT

32c

BRANCHES FOR
DECORATION

HIDING
PLACES

HEATING
MAT

FINE SAND

◆ To raise this gecko properly, it needs to live alone, and you must recreate a little bit of the hot, dry Australian outback.

◆ In the bottom of the terrarium, spread fine sand, preferably red sand, about 1½ inches (3 to 4 cm) deep. These geckos love sand and will roll in it to cover themselves completely. I've never heard of blockages from eating sand in this species, so sand is a must!

◆ The terrarium needs a hot zone and a cool zone. These geckos cannot lower or raise their body temperature by sweating or shivering the way mammals can. They can only regulate their body temperature by moving to the cool zone when they are too hot and heading to the hot zone when they are too cold.

◆ Create the hot zone with a heating lamp above one end of the terrarium or with a heating mat, connected to a thermostat, under one-third of the terrarium. The heating mat is more practical, because it is connected to a thermostat and you can control the temperature: 90° Fahrenheit (32° Celsius) in the hot zone and 77° Fahrenheit (25° Celsius) in the cool zone. At night, lower the temperature to 73° Fahrenheit (23° Celsius).

◆ Put hiding places in both zones. They can be of different kinds: small flowerpots turned upside down, cork bark, reptile shelters from the pet-supply store—whatever you like, as long as your gecko can hide under it.

◆ Lighting on a timer for eleven hours a day in summer and nine hours a day in winter provides a proper day/night cycle for this gecko.

CARE TIPS

These geckos molt (shed their skin) regularly, and I know from experience that this species does not need a molting shelter, as some other geckos do. It molts perfectly well in a dry environment.

FEEDING

• They eat insects and love crickets, along with cockroaches such as red runners. When they're hungry, they will waste no time chasing their prey, with their tails wagging enthusiastically!

• This species does not drink from a dish, so just spray the inside of the terrarium once or twice a week with lukewarm water to keep your gecko hydrated. Spray very lightly—just enough so it can drink the small water droplets, because it really doesn't like humidity.

EASTERN HERMANN'S TORTOISE

Testudo hermanni boettgeri

ALBANIA, TURKEY, MONTENEGRO, BULGARIA, (ROATIA, GREECE, MA(EDONIA

NOTE: ILLEGAL TO SELL IN NEW JERSEY (BUT LEGAL TO KEEP)

CARAPACE (UPPER SHELL)

TAIL

STRONG JAWS

ALL-TERRAIN FEET

PLASTRON (LOWER SHELL)

ORIGIN

Who doesn't like a garden tortoise? This is a truly likable creature.

There are two subspecies of *Testudo hermanni*. The Western Hermann's tortoise, *Testudo hermanni hermanni*, lives in southern France and parts of Italy and Spain, but the subspecies I we will talk about here is *Testudo hermanni boettgeri*, the Eastern Hermann's tortoise, which is easy to find in pet stores. In the wild, it lives in Mediterranean environments that are hot and dry in summer. It hibernates in winter.

Renew items at: www.rockfordpubliclibrary.org

Customer ID: **********6338

Items that you checked out

Title: Can I keep it? : small pets guide
ID: 31112020962102
Due: Monday, June 7, 2021

Total items: 1
Account balance: $0.00
5/17/2021 5:47 PM
Checked out: 1
Overdue: 0
Hold requests: 0
Ready for pickup: 0

Thank you for using the Rockford Public
Library

- The solitary Hermann's tortoise spends its days eating plants and walking long distances.

- It is like the 4-wheel-drive of tortoises with a shell for protection—it is unstoppable! It can even climb if it finds obstacles in its path.

- It's possible, and even quite easy, to keep this species, but you need two essential things: to live in a hot and dry climate and to have an outdoor space, like a yard or garden, where you can build it an enclosure. This species does not live in a terrarium.

- Hermann's tortoises are protected by CITES (Convention on International Trade in Endangered Species of Wild Flora and Fauna), but they can be kept by individuals. Tortoise-keepers in the Unites States are advised to buy captive-bred specimens from United States breeders instead of imported specimens.

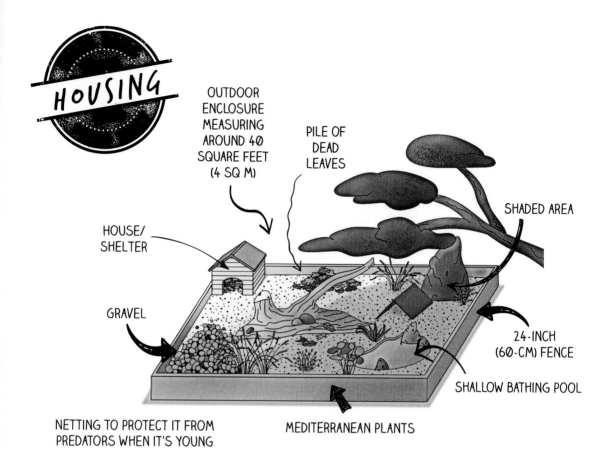

HOUSING

OUTDOOR ENCLOSURE MEASURING AROUND 40 SQUARE FEET (4 SQ M)

PILE OF DEAD LEAVES

SHADED AREA

HOUSE/ SHELTER

GRAVEL

24-INCH (60-CM) FENCE

SHALLOW BATHING POOL

NETTING TO PROTECT IT FROM PREDATORS WHEN IT'S YOUNG

MEDITERRANEAN PLANTS

◆ An enclosure of 40 square feet (4 sq m) is the minimum for an adult. It should have metal mesh that extends 16 inches (40 cm) into the ground, because this turtle digs and may succeed in making an escape tunnel. Because it also climbs easily, you will need a mesh fence or wall at least 24 inches (60 cm) high.

◆ When the tortoise is young, many predators—including cats, birds, and rodents—may try to attack it, so you must put a protective net over the enclosure at the beginning.

◆ The tortoise's home must have sunny areas as well as shady areas where it can go to cool down.

◆ The substrate should be something that drains well, such as smooth gravel. This will prevent puddles of water from forming when it rains. This tortoise does not like humidity.

◆ A house with hay and dry leaves inside will be the perfect place for it to shelter at night and is also essential for its hibernation period.

◆ Use a large, shallow plastic dish as a bathing pool. The tortoise will love it!

◆ Plant Mediterranean plants, such as lavender, and lay a tree trunk in the enclosure. These will add more shade while making your tortoise's home look very attractive.

EASTERN HERMANN'S TORTOISE

FEEDING

- Offer vegetation rich in calcium, such as watercress, lamb's lettuce, and dandelion leaves. This tortoise also loves barbary figs.

- You can buy wild plant-seed mixtures for turtles that you can plant inside the enclosure. The tortoise will enjoy eating the plants.

- In summer, feed your tortoise every day; however, if the enclosure has many edible plants growing in it, you can provide vegetables just a few times a week. The rest of the time, it will manage on its own.

- Sprinkle calcium powder for reptiles on your tortoise's food. It needs calcium to grow.

RAZOR-BACKED MUSK TURTLE

Sternotherus carinatus
(or Kinosternon carinatus)

EASTERN UNITED STATES

NOTE: RESTRICTED IN HAWAII; ILLEGAL TO
SELL IN NEW JERSEY (BUT LEGAL TO KEEP)

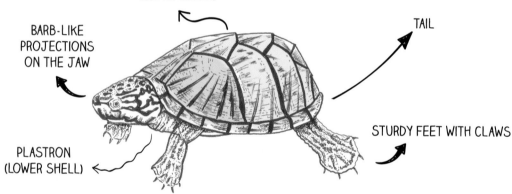

ROOF-SHAPED CARAPACE
(UPPER SHELL)

BARB-LIKE
PROJECTIONS
ON THE JAW

TAIL

STURDY FEET WITH CLAWS

PLASTRON
(LOWER SHELL)

ORIGIN

This aquatic turtle isn't a champion swimmer or hunter. It lives in fairly calm waters in areas with a lot of aquatic plants.

In the wild, it is opportunistic and will eat whatever it can find, including mollusks, slow-moving fish, and aquatic insects. Although it's not the best swimmer, it often walks on the bottom of the pond where it lives.

This is a very interesting-looking turtle, with its roof-shaped shell. It grows to a manageable size in adulthood: about 6 inches (15 cm) long.

BEHAVIOR

- Turtles do not like to be handled and may bite to defend themselves. Watch your fingers!

- If you must handle your turtle—to move it to another spot, for example—wash your hands thoroughly afterward. Turtles can carry salmonella, which is not good for you. It's rare to get sick from a turtle, but it pays to be careful!

MY OBSERVATIONS
Housing for an aquatic turtle is fairly expensive, but you need the right setup if you want your turtle to live comfortably in your home. Be sure to calculate the costs beforehand!

HOUSING

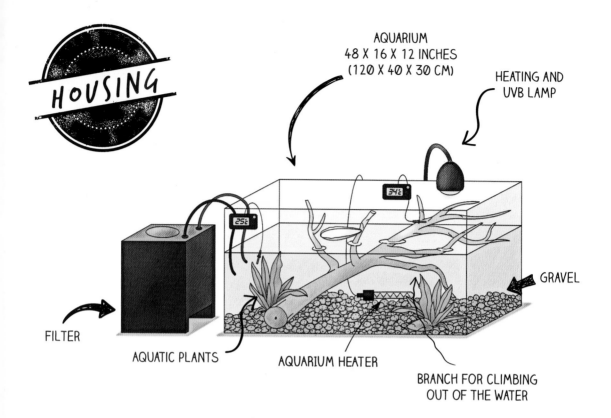

AQUARIUM
48 X 16 X 12 INCHES
(120 X 40 X 30 CM)

HEATING AND
UVB LAMP

GRAVEL

FILTER

AQUATIC PLANTS

AQUARIUM HEATER

BRANCH FOR CLIMBING
OUT OF THE WATER

◆ Like all aquatic turtles, this species needs the right tank setup in order to live comfortably.

◆ Turtles pollute the water as they eat, so you need a good filtration system. It can be a filter inside the tank or an external filter under the aquarium, but, either way, the filter must be large. Clean it once a week.

◆ Use an aquarium heater to keep the water at 75 to 77° Fahrenheit (24 to 25° Celsius).

◆ Your turtle needs to be able to get out of the water and bask in the heat, so provide a branch, a floating beach for turtles, or cork bark on the surface. Over this area, set up a heating lamp to get a precise 90 to 95° Fahrenheit (32 to 35° Celsius) hot spot. Adjust the height of the bulb to achieve the right temperature.

◆ You will also need a bulb that emits UVB rays. UVB is essential for the turtle to absorb calcium and grow properly and is a required part of your aquatic turtle's setup. A 10.0 UVB tube will be perfect. Change it at least once a year—every six months is even better.

◆ Connect the heating lamp and UVB bulb to a timer set to eleven hours per day.

◆ At the bottom of the aquarium, lay gravel. It must be large enough that your turtle won't swallow it while eating, but not too large, or else the waste will not be able to exit through the filter.

◆ Aquatic plants like elodea will provide hiding places that the turtle will like. Add a few flowerpots broken in half so the turtle can hide underneath them.

RAZOR-BACKED MUSK TURTLE

CARE TIPS
Be vigilant about cleaning the filter every week!

FEEDING

• Offer your turtle high-quality pellets for aquatic turtles from a brand that specializes in reptiles, such as Zoo Med or Exo Terra. Add pieces of deboned fish or earthworms from time to time.

• A piece of cuttlebone floating in a corner of the tank will provide calcium if there isn't enough in its diet.

• Feed it six days out of seven. One day of fasting per week won't do your turtle any harm.

AFRICAN WHIP SPIDER

Damon variegatus

TROPICAL AFRICA: SOUTH AFRICA, NAMIBIA, ZIMBABWE, ZAMBIA, MOZAMBIQUE, THE CONGO, TANZANIA

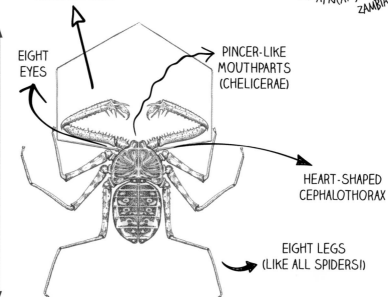

SPINY FORELEGS, CALLED ANTENNIFORM

EIGHT EYES

PINCER-LIKE MOUTHPARTS (CHELICERAE)

BODY SIZE:
2 INCHES (5 CM);
UP TO 10 INCHES
(25 CM) WITH
LEGS UNFOLDED

HEART-SHAPED CEPHALOTHORAX

EIGHT LEGS
(LIKE ALL SPIDERS!)

ORIGIN

Looking like a little monster, the whip spider (also known as the "tailless whip scorpion") must be a real nightmare for some people! But these arachnids are totally harmless. They live in the dark, in caves or on rock faces, in the humid zones of tropical regions.

This spider only uses three out of its four pairs of legs for walking. The legs at the front of its body, which are very delicate, are for feeling and exploring its environment.

- Whip spiders are 100 percent nocturnal, and they do not spin webs. They go out at night in search of prey that they will catch with their long, spiny, raptor-like forelegs.

- They always move vertically and never descend to the ground.

- If you handle your whip spider, do it gently. It is very fragile, especially its long legs.

- Your spider will molt regularly. After it molts, you will find its shed skin, called exuvia—it will look like a perfect double of your pet, but it's only the outer casing!

MY OBSERVATIONS
You will be lucky if you can convince your family to welcome this creature into your home!

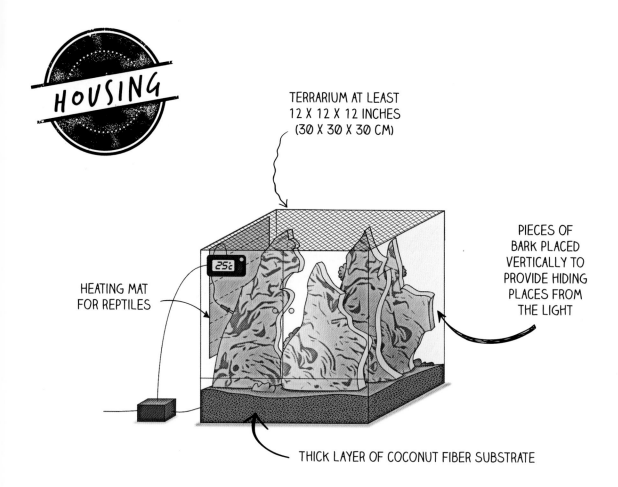

TERRARIUM AT LEAST
12 X 12 X 12 INCHES
(30 X 30 X 30 CM)

PIECES OF
BARK PLACED
VERTICALLY TO
PROVIDE HIDING
PLACES FROM
THE LIGHT

HEATING MAT
FOR REPTILES

25ċ

THICK LAYER OF COCONUT FIBER SUBSTRATE

◆ A terrarium of 12 x 12 x 12 inches (30 x 30 x 30 cm) is the minimum size for one whip spider to live comfortably. Larger is even better.

◆ Place a layer of coconut fiber substrate at the bottom. Keep the substrate damp at all times.

◆ Place pieces of cork bark vertically against the tank walls. Your whip spider will enjoy slipping between the pieces of bark, where it will spend its days out of the light.

◆ Do not light the terrarium. Light will really bother your spider.

◆ Maintain the proper temperature with a small heating mat for reptiles. Do not exceed 77° Fahrenheit (25° Celsius) during the day, and turn it off at night to allow the temperature to drop to 68 to 72° Fahrenheit (20 to 22° Celsius).

◆ Your whip spider needs a really humid environment, so spray the terrarium every day.

CARE TIPS
Providing humidity and the proper temperatures in the tank is very important!

FEEDING

- Offer your spider a few medium-sized crickets once or twice a week.

- Be sure to remove any uneaten prey.

SNAKES

TIPS FOR BEGINNERS

Most snakes are easy animals to raise because they eat only once a week, they don't make noise, and they do not smell bad. Also, the smaller species don't take up a lot of space. In short, snakes make good pets. Here's some information on the basics you need to know about before you decide to get a snake. The species described on the following pages are easy to raise and perfect for beginners.

HOUSING TIPS

→ Run the lighting and heat in your terrarium for a few days to get the temperature right before you bring your snake home.

→ Always place the heating cable or mat outside the tank and always use a thermostat to control the temperature.

→ Make sure your thermostat allows you to lower the temperature by 7 to 9° Fahrenheit (4 to 5° Celsius) at night. This is essential for long-term snake-keeping.

→ Snakes need hiding places to live in peace. Set up as many as possible in the terrarium, because snakes really don't like being out in the open. It causes them a lot of stress. Some options are pieces of cork bark turned upside down and plastic plants.

→ Change their water at least every two days. Reptiles like fresh water.

→ Change the substrate regularly.

- When your snake's eyes are blue, it means it's going to molt (shed its skin). Don't feed it at this time. Wait until it has finished molting to feed it.

- Let your snake adapt to its new home for a few days before you try to handle it for the first time. Reptiles generally don't like to be handled, so if you take it out of its terrarium, it's for your own enjoyment, not your snake's.

- Always handle your snake by supporting it in two places on its body, never for more than twenty minutes at a time, and at a comfortable temperature for the snake (for example, never lay it on a cold floor in the wintertime!).

- Wash your hands with soap and use hand sanitizer before and after handling your snake.

FEEDING TIPS

- Feed your snake thawed prey that is suitable for its size. Giving your snake a live animal is a bad idea—the prey animal will be stressed and may bite the snake. It's not a good situation for either one of them!

- You can find the type of prey you need at pet-supply stores and from specialty online sellers.

- Make sure you completely thaw out the prey by letting it soak in hot water. Dry it with paper towels and then dangle it in front of the snake's face with special feeding tongs available at pet-supply stores.

- Increase the size of the prey as your snake grows. A young grass snake starts by eating tiny mice at birth, and then it eats adult mice once it has reached adult size.

- Do not overfeed your snake. Many snakes in captivity get a little too fat. One meal per week for a young snake is sufficient. One meal every ten to fifteen days for an adult snake is plenty. Obesity tends to shorten a snake's life, just like it does for us.

- If your snake refuses its prey, don't panic. Snakes often fast (go without eating for a period of time). Instead, offer your snake something new to eat a few days later (you can't refreeze prey once it has thawed). Some species, such as ball pythons, can fast for months in winter without harming their health.

MY OBSERVATIONS
I almost forgot to tell you: snakes are masters of escape. Always be careful to close the terrarium properly!

CORN SNAKE

Pantherophis guttatus

SOUTHEASTERN UNITED STATES

NOTE: ILLEGAL TO KEEP IN HAWAII AND GEORGIA; ONLY CERTAIN COLOR MORPHS ARE LEGAL IN NEW JERSEY WITH PERMIT

BEHAVIOR

- This is one of the most popular pet snakes as well as the most widely bred species.

- it is a reasonable size at 4 feet (1.2 m), it has a calm personality and a good appetite, and it comes in hundreds of different colors as the result of selective breeding in captivity.

MY OBSERVATIONS
This species is often recommended for beginners. A child as young as ten can take care of it properly.

CORN SNAKE

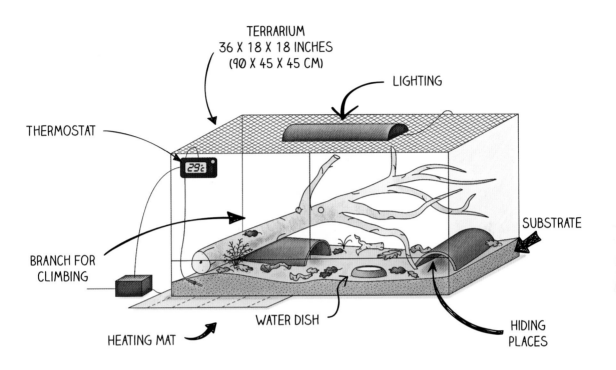

TERRARIUM
36 X 18 X 18 INCHES
(90 X 45 X 45 CM)

LIGHTING

THERMOSTAT

29°c

BRANCH FOR
CLIMBING

SUBSTRATE

HEATING MAT

WATER DISH

HIDING
PLACES

HOUSING

➡ An 84° Fahrenheit (29° Celsius) hot zone and a 75° Fahrenheit (24° Celsius) cool zone will help it regulate its own temperature in the terrarium.

➡ A substrate of coconut fiber, kept dry, or aspen snake bedding will be perfect.

FEEDING

• If you feed your corn snake rodents correctly, it will grow quickly and shouldn't be difficult to raise.

KINGSNAKE

Lampropeltis sp.

SOUTHERN NORTH AMERICA, CENTRAL AMERICA, NORTHERN SOUTH AMERICA

NOTE: ILLEGAL TO KEEP IN HAWAII AND GEORGIA

BEHAVIOR

- Kingsnakes are very attractive because of their bright colors.

- Many different kingsnake species are available in captivity. Some of their colors imitate the fearsome coral snake, but kingsnakes are completely harmless grass snakes.

- These snakes are not too big at about 32 inches (80 cm).

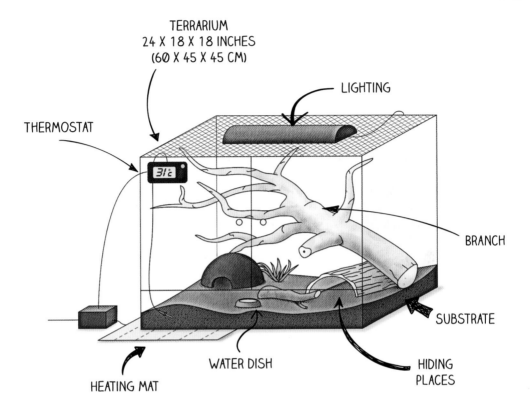

TERRARIUM
24 X 18 X 18 INCHES
(60 X 45 X 45 CM)

LIGHTING

THERMOSTAT

31°c

BRANCH

SUBSTRATE

WATER DISH

HIDING
PLACES

HEATING MAT

HOUSING

♦ An 88° Fahrenheit (31° Celsius) hot zone will be appreciated, along with a 77° Fahrenheit (25° Celsius) cool zone.

♦ Like all snakes, the kingsnake needs plenty of hiding places in its habitat.

♦ Keep the substrate dry. Use aspen snake bedding, coconut fiber, or even a mixture of coconut fiber and sand.

FEEDING

• Kingsnakes are big eaters and will sometimes mistake your fingers for prey when you open the terrarium. Don't panic—its bite is completely harmless!

• To prevent your snake from trying to eat your fingers, get it used to eating from a container that you set aside specially for its food.

GARTER SNAKE

Thamnophis sp.

CANADA,
UNITED
STATES

NOTE: ILLEGAL TO KEEP IN
HAWAII, GEORGIA, AND NEW YORK

BEHAVIOR

- Garter snakes are a little different from other grass snakes because they eat fish. This snake is a good choice if your family doesn't like the idea of storing mice in the freezer!

- These snakes are awake during the day and are very active in their terrariums, so proper habitat is essential.

- Your garter snake may not like to be handled and can react by "musking"—releasing a bad-smelling odor onto the person trying to handle it. Don't say I didn't warn you!

GARTER SNAKE

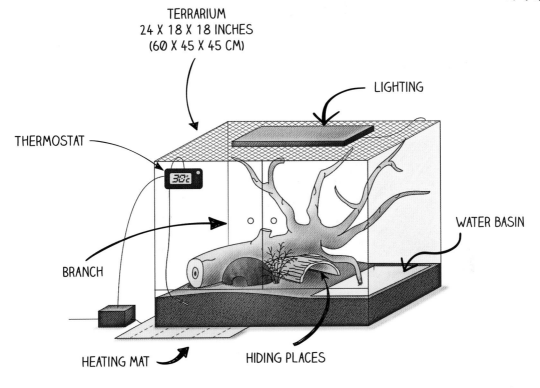

TERRARIUM
24 X 18 X 18 INCHES
(60 X 45 X 45 CM)

LIGHTING

THERMOSTAT

30c

WATER BASIN

BRANCH

HEATING MAT

HIDING PLACES

HOUSING

▶ Your garter snake will like having a basin of water for bathing. Change the water several times a week.

▶ An 86° Fahrenheit (30° Celsius) hot zone and a 75° Fahrenheit (24° Celsius) cool zone is important. The water basin should be in the cool zone to prevent the water from heating up, which would allow bacteria to grow very quickly.

FEEDING

• Pet garter snakes eat mainly thawed rodents, particularly mice, but you can vary your snake's diet.

• If you feed your garter snake fish or frogs' legs, buy them frozen and thaw before feeding. Freezing kills parasites, so it's best to buy frozen varieties of this food.

• Don't feed your garter snake ocean fish or goldfish. They contain a substance called thiaminase, which is not good for your snake.

THAI RED MOUNTAIN RAT SNAKE

Oreocryptophis porphyraceus coxi

NORTHERN THAILAND

NOTE: ILLEGAL TO KEEP IN HAWAII AND GEORGIA

BEHAVIOR

- This is my favorite snake! It's a real beauty—orange with two black stripes on its back.

- This species stays buried in its substrate during the day and only comes out at night to hunt.

- It's very easy to raise and pretty inexpensive to set up, because it lives in a cooler environment and doesn't like the heat.

MY OBSERVATIONS
Some of these snakes tolerate being handled, but others do not like it at all. You'll figure this out with your own individual snake.

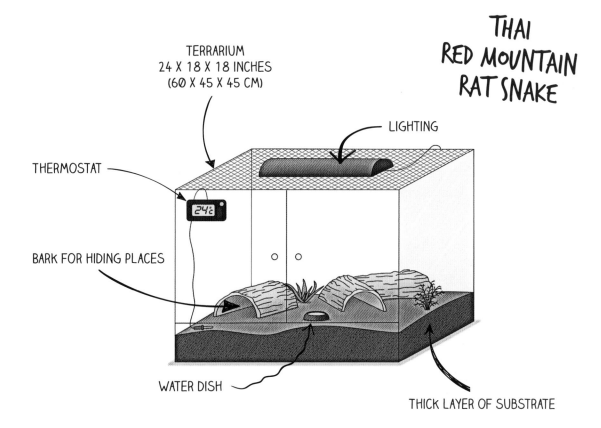

THAI RED MOUNTAIN RAT SNAKE

TERRARIUM
24 X 18 X 18 INCHES
(60 X 45 X 45 CM)

LIGHTING

THERMOSTAT

BARK FOR HIDING PLACES

WATER DISH

THICK LAYER OF SUBSTRATE

HOUSING

◆ A temperature of 72 to 75° Fahrenheit (22 to 24° Celsius) is perfect. Lay a thick layer of substrate at the bottom, 2 to 3 inches (5 to 8 cm) deep. A mixture of 70 percent coconut fiber and 30 percent ground sphagnum moss will do the job.

◆ Keep half the substrate slightly damp by spraying it regularly, and leave the other half dry.

◆ Lay pieces of cork bark for hiding places.

◆ Install lighting that uses energy-saving bulbs. This will be enough to heat the terrarium for this species.

FEEDING

• It is easy to feed this snake rodents that are suitable for its size.

CRESTED GECKO

Correlophus ciliates

NEW CALEDONIA

NOTE: ILLEGAL TO KEEP IN HAWAII

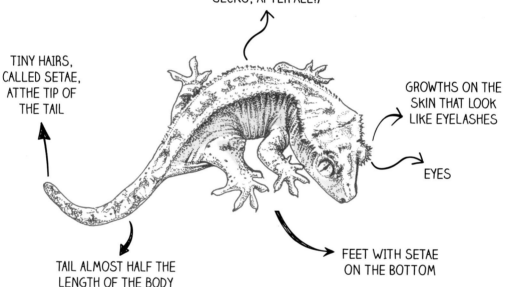

CREST (IT'S CALLED THE CRESTED GECKO, AFTER ALL!)

TINY HAIRS, CALLED SETAE, AT THE TIP OF THE TAIL

GROWTHS ON THE SKIN THAT LOOK LIKE EYELASHES

EYES

TAIL ALMOST HALF THE LENGTH OF THE BODY

FEET WITH SETAE ON THE BOTTOM

ORIGIN

This gecko lives in trees in the wild. This species is endemic to New Caledonia, meaning that it is the only place where this gecko is found in the wild. The species was thought to be extinct before being rediscovered in 1994. Since then, it has been bred on a large scale in captivity. The crested geckos sold as pets have been captive-bred.

- The crested gecko is both a frugivore (fruit-eater) and an insectivore (insect-eater). The fact that it lives in cooler temperatures makes it easier and more economical to raise, so it's a great species for beginners to start with.

- Some people think that tree-dwelling geckos have suction cups on the bottoms of their feet, but they are actually hairs! Setae are microscopic (very tiny), very dense hairs that stick to all surfaces, allowing the gecko to walk upside down.

- This gecko even has setae on the tip of its tail. The tail is prehensile, meaning it can grasp and hold objects, and the gecko can cling to an object by rolling its tail around it.

- The crested gecko is a champion long-jumper. With almost no warning, it will jump forward, four legs spread, to land at a distance, where it can cling to a surface thanks to the setae under its feet.

MY OBSERVATIONS

This species is really charming and attractive. Crested geckos raised in captivity come in many different colors.

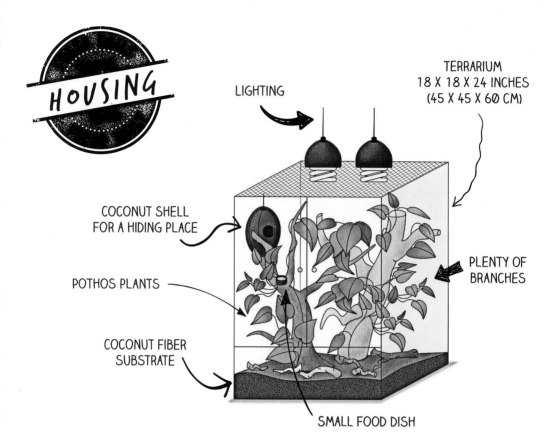

HOUSING

LIGHTING

TERRARIUM
18 X 18 X 24 INCHES
(45 X 45 X 60 CM)

COCONUT SHELL
FOR A HIDING PLACE

POTHOS PLANTS

COCONUT FIBER
SUBSTRATE

PLENTY OF
BRANCHES

SMALL FOOD DISH

◆ The crested gecko is a tree-dweller, so it will need a fairly tall terrarium. A tank measuring 18 x 18 x 24 inches (45 x 45 x 60 cm) is perfect for one gecko.

◆ At the bottom, spread coconut fiber, and keep it slightly damp. Place plenty of branches that reach from the bottom to the top of the terrarium. These will allow the gecko to climb and give it places to rest. Using branches of different thicknesses imitates what the gecko would find in the wild.

◆ Pothos is a climbing plant that will wind itself around the branches and make the terrarium look more like a jungle.

◆ Lighting at the top will help the plants thrive. I suggest using two different types of light: an energy-saving bulb for the plants and another bulb with 5 percent UVB. From experience, I know that UVB rays are good for these geckos, even if they aren't a requirement.

◆ The crested gecko lives in cooler conditions than many other reptiles—and that's good for your electric bill! A room temperature of 73° Fahrenheit (23° Celsius) will be perfect.

◆ If your gecko ever wants to get warmer, it will move closer to the lamps, where it will find enough heat.

◆ Every evening, spray the entire terrarium to create humidity cycles. At night, there will be high humidity in the tank, and then the terrarium will dry out during the day until the next time you spray. Maintaining high humidity twenty-four hours a day is not good for your gecko.

◆ If you set up your terrarium properly, you'll have a miniature jungle in your home!

CARE TIPS

You can handle your gecko gently from time to time, but never catch or hold it by its tail, which can break off in your hand and never grow back. If this does happen, the gecko can continue to live comfortably without its tail. Most specimens in the wild lose their tails.

FEEDING

• Feed your gecko mashed fruit in a small dish placed in the branches.

• Change the fruit every evening at bedtime. You can vary the type of fruit and see what it likes best.

• Twice a week, give your gecko a few crickets to hunt. Once a week, sprinkle the crickets with calcium powder for reptiles. It's very important for your gecko's growth and health.

• There are also several brands of crested gecko food in powder form. You mix it with water, and it's a very good source of complete nutrition. But be warned: geckos often get hooked on it and may become picky about eating regular mashed fruit.

WHAT YOU SHOULD KNOW

In this book, I've presented thirty-nine very special species of animal. Many of these species are considered "exotic" pets. In the United States, there are federal, state, county, and municipal laws governing the keeping and breeding of animals. In some cases, certain animals cannot travel from state to state, which can make out-of-state purchasing complicated.

Before deciding on one of these pets, do your homework so that you know the laws in your area and find a licensed breeder or pet store that sells the animal you are interested in. Also, as the future owner of an exotic pet, it's important for you to understand animal rights. A major document that governs the sale, breeding, and ownership of animals around the world is the Convention on International Trade in Endangered Species of Wild Flora and Fauna (CITES) (cites.org). Also known as the Washington Convention, it has helped protect animals by controlling the trade of different species around the world since 1975.

In this book, we have listed restrictions on ownership that apply to certain species, but laws change, and we recommend checking with the US Fish and Wildlife Service as well as individual state offices for the most current regulations before purchasing exotic pets. Also remember that you must monitor your pets' health and ensure their well-being, which requires thorough knowledge of their species. If you do not take care of your animals, you can be prosecuted.

TAKING CARE OF YOUR PET

You can never release your pet into the wild. Your animal was born in captivity, and it is not prepared for life in the wild. It may not survive very long, especially because the climate and other conditions where you live probably are not the same as its natural environment.

Releasing the animal into the wild is dangerous both for your animal and for local species because it can upset the local ecosystem. For example, the spiny-cheek crayfish (*Orconectes limosus*) is an American species that was introduced to Europe in the 1890s. Scientists soon discovered that this species was more resistant to disease and pollution than the local white-clawed crayfish (*Austropotamobius pallipes*), which is now an endangered species, and the European crayfish (*Astacus astacus*). When spiny-cheek crayfish invaded the environment, they began competing with the local crayfish species for food, leading to the disappearance of the local species!

REMEMBER THAT YOUR ANIMAL WILL GROW!

WHERE CAN YOU FIND THESE ANIMALS?

Look for local pet stores that have a good reputation. Some pets, such as hamsters, gerbils, and geckos, will be easier to find. For other species, you may have to visit a store that specializes in exotic pets. If you prefer to find specialized breeders, you will find contacts by looking for information about your chosen species online. In many cases, if you cannot find a local breeder, you will be able to find a breeder online who can ship your pet safely to you.

As for equipment, again start out at your local pet store. If your budget is limited, check out Facebook groups or Craigslist for used equipment. You may be able to find what you need at lower prices.

THE ADVENTURE BEGINS

Again, I advise you to think very carefully before you adopt an animal. Your decision to bring home a new pet must be carefully considered and accepted by everyone living in your home. In some cases, you will need a little luck to convince your family to welcome one of these unusual creatures! I previously mentioned that you must plan ahead for unexpected circumstances: behavior problems, moving, financial difficulties, and so forth. Also know the expected life span of the animal you want. Keeping a fighting fish for three years is not the same as caring for a bullfrog for ten years!

Who will care for your pet when you are away? You have some options. Before you travel, recruit family or friends to take care of your pet, hire a pet sitter, or find people with whom you can do a free pet-sitting exchange by offering to take care of their pet in the future.

Now you have the key information you need to adopt one of the animals in this book. Good luck!

WHERE DID THE PRAYING MANTIS GO?

The French publisher would like to thank the entire team of La Ferme Tropicale (54 rue Jenner, Paris, France) for their warm welcome.

PHOTO CREDITS

ABOUT THE AUTHOR

Passionate about animals from an early age, Tanguy had the opportunity to make animals his profession. He has been an animal wrangler in the movie industry and has worked alongside French television host Christophe Dechavanne on many of his programs. Tanguy went on to create Toopet, the first French YouTube channel dedicated entirely to animals. Dogs, snakes, chickens, hamsters—you can find (almost!) every animal on Toopet.